EmSAT Chemistry
Achieve

First edition

EmSAT Chemistry Achieve

Dr Sinclair Steele

Academic Medical Press

Published by Academic Medical Press, Preston, UK.

Academic Medical Press.
88005 York House, Green Lane West, Preston, PR3 1NJ
Somniare audemus

Copyright © Dr S. Steele 2021

All rights reserved. No part of this publication may be reproduced or transmitted in any form or by any means, electronically or mechanically, including photocopying, recording or any information storage or retrieval system, without prior permission in writing from the publisher.

This work is registered with the UK Copyright Service: Registration No:
284741446

First published 2021

Whilst the advice and information in this book are believed to be true and accurate at the date of going to press, neither the author nor the publisher can accept any legal responsibility or liability for any errors or omissions that may be made.

Any websites referred to in this publication are in the public domain and their addresses are provided by Academic Medical Press for information only. Academic Medical Press disclaims any responsibility for the content.

ISBN 978-0-9566443-8-1

Further copies can be obtained from: www.academicmedicalpress.com
                                       http://www.lulu.com
                                       http://www.amazon.com

Preface to the first edition

As an experienced educator I have noticed that one of the issues that frequently concerns good students is the lack of practice questions for important examinations. The EmSAT, which is this country's version of the SAT, is a comparatively new exam in the UAE and suffers from this same issue. So, I was moved to write high quality questions, answers and explanations to satisfy the needs of the students preparing to sit the EmSAT.

The significance of the EmSAT Chemistry Achieve examination is that it is a baseline requirement for attending university in the UAE, particularly if the student is planning to take a degree in chemistry or a related subject. Scores of the order of 1200 - 1400 and above are good indications of likely success in a candidate's application to university. The judicious use of the questions in this text for practice as the EmSAT exam approaches should sharpen skills and significantly improve exam scores in such students.

This book includes six chapters of complete mock examination questions and covers all of the question types and subject areas tested in the authentic examination. The form and standard of the exams are equivalent to the real EmSAT Chemistry Achieve exam.

I would like to thank my colleagues in the UAE and the UK for their support in the completion of this text. I would also like to offer special thanks to my diligent and patient editor – *Abdus Samad Soliman*. I am extremely grateful for his assistance.

Dubai, June 2021
Dr Sinclair Steele
Associate Professor

CONTENTS

Chapter 1
EmSAT Test 1   1 - 10
Answers   11 - 24

Chapter 2
EmSAT Test 2   25 - 34
Answers   35 - 46

Chapter 3
EmSAT Test 3   47 - 55
Answers   56 - 67

Chapter 4
EmSAT Test 4   68 - 77
Answers   78 - 89

Chapter 5
EmSAT Test 5   90 - 98
Answers   99 - 111

Chapter 6
EmSAT Test 6   112 - 120
Answers   121 - 134

Page(s)

Test One

1. Compared to the charge on a neutron the electron's charge is:

○ A. Greater and the same sign.
○ B. Equal and the same sign.
○ C. Greater and positive.
○ D. Greater and negative.

2. The mass number of an atom is equal to the number of:

○ A. Protons and electrons in the nucleus.
○ B. Neutrons and electrons in the nucleus.
○ C. Protons and neutrons in the nucleus.
○ D. Protons and electrons in the ion.

3. What is the total number of electrons shared in the C=O bond in the benzoic acid molecule shown below?

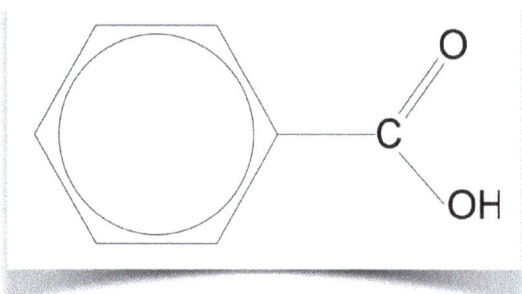

○ A. One
○ B. Two
○ C. Three
○ D. Four

4. For the nuclear reaction below which of the nuclide options represents the unknown nuclide X?

○ A. $^{28}_{13}Al$
○ B. $^{29}_{14}Al$
○ C. $^{26}_{13}Al$
○ D. $^{27}_{14}Al$

5. Thomson's beam experiments were the first to show:

○ A. That a negatively charged subatomic particle existed.
○ B. That protons existed.
○ C. That neutrons existed.
○ D. That the nucleus existed.

6. Silicon has an atomic number of 14 and its electronic configuration is $1s^2 2s^2 2p^6 3s^2 3p^2$. Aluminium has an atomic number of 13. What is aluminium's electronic configuration?

○ A. $1s^2 2s^2 2p^6 3s^2 3p^2$
○ B. $1s^2 2s^2 2p^6 3s^2 3p^4$
○ C. $1s^2 2s^2 2p^6 3s^2 3p^1$
○ D. $1s^2 2s^2 2p^6 3s^2 3p^3$

7. Each column in the periodic table is a:

○ A. Group
○ B. Period
○ C. Diagonal
○ D. Horizontal

8. A solid changes state and becomes liquid. What is this process called?

○ A. Sublimation
○ B. Melting
○ C. Evaporating
○ D. Freezing

9. "The volume of a gas is inversely proportional to its pressure, if the number of gas particles and the temperature are constant." This is a description of:

○ A. Boyle's law
○ B. Charles' law
○ C. Newton's law
○ D. Faraday's law

10. Which of the following is the most reactive element?

○ A. Neon
○ B. Helium
○ C. Potassium
○ D. Argon

11. Which of the following is the most reactive Group IA element?

- A. Sodium
- B. Potassium
- C. Lithium
- D. Caesium

12. A student is using the alkali $KOH_{(aq)}$ to neutralize the acid $HNO_{3(aq)}$. 50 ml of 50 mM of $KOH_{(aq)}$ is required to neutralize 25 ml of $HNO_{3(aq)}$. What is the concentration of the $HNO_{3(aq)}$ in mM?

- A. 50 mM
- B. 100 mM
- C. 200 mM
- D. 300 mM

13. Which of the following is the description of a liquid?

- A. The opposite state of matter to a plasma.
- B. The state of matter in which a material has neither a definite shape nor a definite volume.
- C. The state of matter in which a material has a definite volume and a definite shape.
- D. The state of matter in which a material has a definite volume but not a definite shape.

14.

$$A_{(aq)} \rightleftharpoons B_{(aq)}$$

The correct expression for calculating the equilibrium constant for the above reaction at equilibrium in water is:

- A. $K_{eq} = [A]/[B]$
- B. $K_{eq} = [B]/[A]$
- C. $K_{eq} = [A] \times [B]$
- D. $K_{eq} = [B]-[A]$

15. A liquid contains a solute that does not separate out. This liquid can be poured through a filter unchanged and this liquid allows light to pass through it clearly. This liquid is a:

- A. Solution
- B. Suspension
- C. Colloid
- D. Solid

16. Liquid mixtures can be separated by distillation because of their different:

- A. Melting points
- B. Boiling points
- C. Solidifying points
- D. Condensation points

17. Sodium chloride has a mass of 58.44 g per mole. How many grams of sodium chloride must be completely dissolved in a 500 ml of water to make a 1 molar solution?

- A. 116.88 g
- B. 58.44 g
- C. 29.22 g
- D. 14.61 g

18. Isotopes are:

- A. Elements that have nuclei with different numbers of neutrons.
- B. Elements that have nuclei with different numbers of protons.
- C. Radioactive.
- D. Chemically reactive.

19. The number of neutrons in the nucleus of an atom is equal to:

- A. The mass number minus the atomic number.
- B. The atomic number minus the mass number.
- C. The total number of electrons.
- D. The total number of protons.

20. A joule is a measure of:

- A. Pressure
- B. Mass
- C. Volume
- D. Energy

21. Which of the following processes is an example of *deposition*?

- A. Liquid to solid - freezing water on a cold day.
- B. Solid to gas - iodine solid to iodine vapour.
- C. Gas to solid - water vapour forming frost on a cold window.
- D. Liquid to gas - water to steam (water vapour).

22. Metals are:

○ A. Bad conductors of heat.
○ B. Bad conductors of electricity.
○ C. Not reactive.
○ D. Good conductors of electricity.

23. Which element is a soft metal that can be cut with a knife, is very reactive, reacts with cold water and is usually stored under oil?

○ A. Chlorine
○ B. Iron
○ C. Sodium
○ D. Neon

24. Which statement about the modern periodic table is true?

○ A. The elements are listed in the sequence of their mass numbers.
○ B. The elements are listed in the sequence of their atomic numbers.
○ C. Only metals are shown.
○ D. Only non-metals are shown.

25. At normal room temperature and pressure hydrogen is a:

○ A. Gas
○ B. Liquid
○ C. Solid
○ D. Plasma

26. A student mixes two elements together and a chemical reaction occurs that produces heat. The reaction is:

○ A. Endothermic
○ B. Exothermic
○ C. Endocaloric
○ D. Exocaloric

27. Which subatomic particle has the smallest mass?

○ A. Electron
○ B. Proton
○ C. Neutron
○ D. Alpha particle

28. At 25 °C an aqueous solution of a 1 M CH₃COOH tested using a universal indicator shows that the pH is 5. This solution is:

○ A. Basic
○ B. Alkaline
○ C. Acidic
○ D. Neutral

$$NaCl_{(aq)} + AgNO_{3(aq)} \longrightarrow NaNO_{3(aq)} + AgCl_{(s)}$$

29. The reaction above is an example of a:

○ A. Direct combination / synthesis reaction
○ B. Single displacement reaction
○ C. Double displacement reaction
○ D. Decomposition reaction

30. The half-life of C-14 (Carbon-14) is 5,700 years. If an ancient wooden weapon has a C-14 content of only 25% of modern wood, how old is the ancient wooden weapon?

○ A. 2,850 years
○ B. 5,700 years
○ C. 8,550 years
○ D. 11,400 years

31. *The atomic mass* of an element is:

○ A. The weighted average of its isotopic masses.
○ B. The number of protons and neutrons in the nucleus.
○ C. The mass of the heaviest isotope.
○ D. The mass of the lightest isotope.

32. The periodic table's Group VIIIA elements are colourless and odourless gases. They are very unreactive. These elements are also called:

○ A. Noble gases
○ B. Metalloids
○ C. Halogens
○ D. Alkaline earth metals

33. When solid iodine crystals are heated a violet gas is produced. This is an example of:

○ A. Deposition
○ B. Sublimation

- C. Melting
- D. Boiling

34. Which of the following is likely to be the best conductor of heat?

- A. Sulphur
- B. Copper
- C. Nitrogen
- D. Carbon

35. Which of the following statements about solid magnesium chloride is not true?

- A. It is an ionic compound.
- B. It has a high melting point.
- C. It contains covalent bonds.
- D. It is a good conductor of electricity when melted.

36. The calcium in calcium chloride is in which form?

- A. Ca^+
- B. Ca^{2+}
- C. Ca^{3+}
- D. Ca^{4+}

37. **OH^-** is called:

- A. Acetate
- B. Hydroxide
- C. Peroxide
- D. Ammonium

38. An alloy is a:

- A. Mixture
- B. Non-metal
- C. Compound
- D. Gas

39. A student is asked to weigh out a mole of chlorobenzene (C_6H_5Cl). This will contain:

- A. Two moles of chlorine atoms.
- B. 6.02×10^{23} molecules of chlorobenzene.

- C. Four moles of hydrogen atoms.
- D. 6.02×10^{22} of atoms of chlorine.

40. Which item in the redox reaction below becomes oxidized?

$$HgCl_{2(aq)} + Sn^{2+}_{(aq)} \longrightarrow Sn^{4+}_{(aq)} + Hg_2Cl_{2(s)} + Cl^-_{(aq)}$$

- A. $HgCl_2$
- B. Hg_2Cl_2
- C. Sn^{2+}
- D. Sn^{4+}

41. According to Dalton's Atomic Theory which of the following is incorrect?

- A. All elements are composed of atoms.
- B. All elements have different masses.
- C. In a compound the proportion or ratio of elements is always constant.
- D. There is no limit to the number of times substances can be divided.

42. Which statement about chemical equilibria is incorrect?

- A. At equilibrium the forward reaction rate equals and balances the reverse reaction rate.
- B. The stable equilibrium state can be reached starting with either reactants or products.
- C. At equilibrium, the concentration of reactants and products remain constant.
- D. Chemical equilibrium can only be reached by starting with substances on the reactant side of the equation.

43. In which family does the element beryllium belong?

- A. Transition elements
- B. Alkaline earth metals
- C. Alkali metals
- D. Inert gases

44. To completely balance the chemical equation below, what is the smallest whole number that must be placed before O_2 so that all of the elements may be balanced using whole numbers?

$$C_2H_6 + \underline{} O_2 \longrightarrow CO_2 + H_2O$$

- A. 3
- B. 4
- C. 6
- D. 7

45. Which of the graphs below showing the energy change during chemical reactions, displays the *most exothermic reaction*?
(R = reactants, P = products; the ordinate/vertical axis measures energy/enthalpy, the abscissa/horizontal axis represents time).

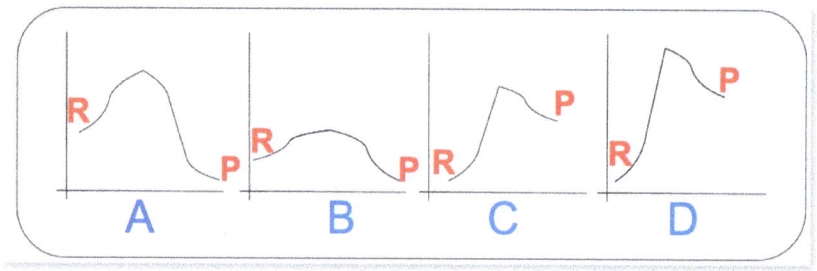

- A. A
- B. B
- C. C
- D. D

46. Which of the options below is the correct description of the ideal gas equation?

- A. P/V=nRT
- B. P/V=mRT
- C. PV=mRT
- D. PV=nRT

47. What is the maximum possible number of electrons in the *p* subshell of an atom?

- A. 2
- B. 4
- C. 6
- D. 8

48. What is the correct equilibrium constant expression (K_{eq}) for the reaction below?

$$4HCl_{(g)} + O_{2(g)} \rightleftharpoons 2H_2O_{(g)} + Cl_{2(g)}$$

- A. $K_{eq} = [H_2O]^2 \times [Cl_2] / [HCl]^4 \times [O_2]$
- B. $K_{eq} = [H_2O] \times [Cl_2] / [HCl] \times [O_2]$
- C. $K_{eq} = 2[H_2O] \times [Cl_2] / 4[HCl] \times [O_2]$
- D. $K_{eq} = [HCl] \times [O_2] / [H_2O] \times [Cl_2]$

49. Sodium reacts with chlorine to make sodium chloride. What type of chemical reaction is this?

○ A. Single displacement
○ B. Decomposition
○ C. Combustion
○ D. Synthesis

50. A molecule is not:

○ A. Polyatomic
○ B. Composed of covalently bonded atoms
○ C. Charged
○ D. Water soluble

TEST ONE

ANSWER SECTION

Test One - Answer Key									
1)	D	11)	D	21)	C	31)	A	41)	D
2)	C	12)	B	22)	D	32)	A	42)	D
3)	D	13)	D	23)	C	33)	B	43)	B
4)	A	14)	B	24)	B	34)	B	44)	D
5)	A	15)	A	25)	A	35)	C	45)	A
6)	C	16)	B	26)	B	36)	B	46)	D
7)	A	17)	C	27)	A	37)	B	47)	C
8)	B	18)	A	28)	C	38)	A	48)	A
9)	A	19)	A	29)	C	39)	B	49)	D
10)	C	20)	D	30)	D	40)	C	50)	C

1. D
An electron has a **greater** and more **negative** charge than a neutron.

An electron has one unit of negative charge whereas a neutron has no charge - so the electron is more negative than the neutron.

The intelligent reader should realize that a similar question could have been asked comparing protons and neutrons or comparing electrons with protons. When preparing for an important exam always consider logical variations of the question you are considering - and how you might answer them!

2. C
The mass number of an atom is equal to the number of **protons and neutrons** in the atom's nucleus.

The mass **number** is always a whole *number*. The mass number is important because it accounts for almost all of the mass of the atom - the electrons add negligible additional mass. Some students confuse mass number with atomic mass. Atomic mass is the average mass of all the nuclei of the element, which includes the different isotopes. Because the atomic mass is an average of isotopic nuclei *it may not be a whole number*.

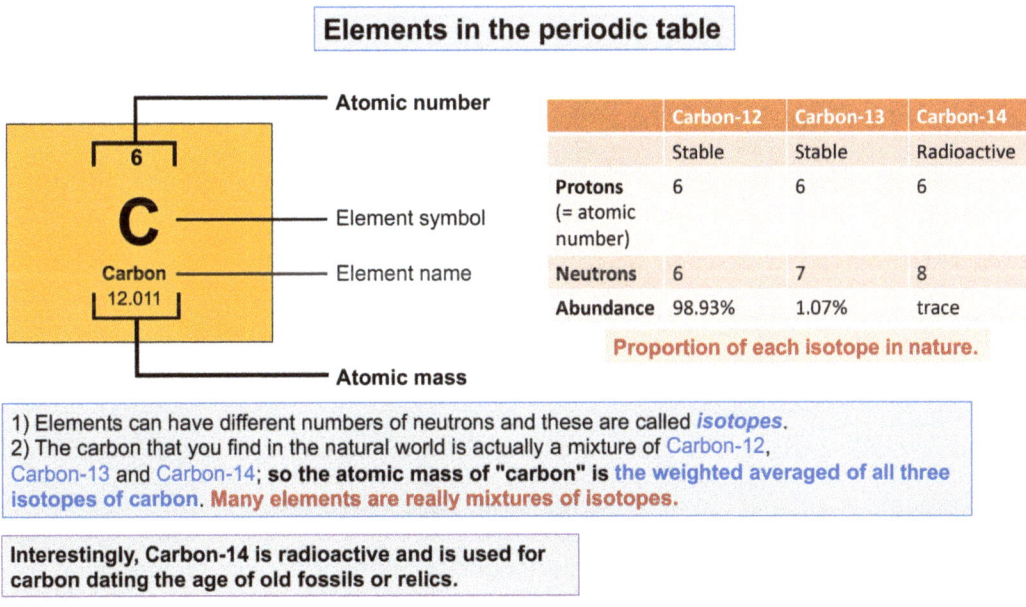

1) Elements can have different numbers of neutrons and these are called *isotopes*.
2) The carbon that you find in the natural world is actually a mixture of Carbon-12, Carbon-13 and Carbon-14; **so the atomic mass of "carbon" is** the weighted averaged of all three isotopes of carbon. **Many elements are really mixtures of isotopes.**

Interestingly, Carbon-14 is radioactive and is used for carbon dating the age of old fossils or relics.

3. D
The total number of electrons shared in the C=O bond in the benzoic acid molecule is *four*.

The C=O bond is a double covalent bond. Each covalent bond is a shared pair of electrons, so a double covalent bond must have four shared electrons between the carbon and the oxygen atoms. By similar reasoning a triple covalent bond would have six shared electrons.

4. A

The correct answer is $^{28}_{13}Al$ (Aluminium-28).

The answer can be calculated by making sure that the total of the mass numbers ("A") on the left side of the equation (25+4=29) equals the total of the mass numbers on the right side of the equation (1+28=29). Similarly, the number of protons ("Z") on left side of the equation (12+2=14) must balance the number on the right (1+13=14):

$$^{25}_{12}Mg + ^{4}_{2}He \longrightarrow ^{1}_{1}H + ^{28}_{13}Al$$

5. A

Thomson's beam experiments were the first to show that **negatively** charged subatomic particles existed.

Thomson's experiment was able to show that a new beam of subatomic particles that he had produced were deflected away from a negative charge and towards a positive charge. This demonstrated that the new particles were negatively charged.

A student revising for the EmSAT chemistry exam would be wise to review the different models of the atom and the evidence for each model.

6. C

The correct answer is **$1s^2 2s^2 2p^6 3s^2 3p^1$**.

To answer this question the sequence of filling of atomic subshells by electrons needs to be known and the number of electrons that are in the atom must also be known. Fortunately, this information is available because the electronic configuration of silicon is given in the question stem. In addition, aluminium's atomic number of 13 means that the atom must contain 13 protons - and *must also contain 13 electrons* for the atom to be neutrally charged.

The "s" subshells can take a maximum of two electrons and the "p" subshells can take a maximum of six electrons. So the unexcited state of the atom must have the 13 electrons in the sequence: $1s^2 2s^2 2p^6 3s^2 3p^1$.

7. A

By convention the vertical columns in the periodic table are called **groups**.

These groups are important in chemistry because they contain elements of similar chemical properties. The groups have numerical names and also family names (for example group 7A is also called the *halogens*). In contrast, the horizontal rows in the periodic table are called *periods* not groups.

8. B

The process of a solid changing state to become a liquid is called **melting**.

Phase Change	Example	Terminology (Name)
solid to liquid	Ice to water.	Melting
liquid to gas	Water to steam (water vapour).	Evaporation / Vaporization
solid to gas	1) Iodine solid to iodine vapour. 2) Dry ice (solid CO_2) to carbon dioxide gas.	Sublimation
gas to liquid	Condensation that occurs to cause rain.	Condensation
liquid to solid	Freezing of water to form ice on a cold day.	Freezing
gas to solid	Water vapour forming frost on a window.	Deposition

Sublimation is the process of a solid directly transforming into a gas, without going through the liquid phase. *Evaporation* is the process of turning from a liquid to a gas. *Freezing* is the process of changing state from a liquid to a solid:

9. A

Boyle's law states that the **volume of a gas is inversely proportional to its pressure**, if the temperature and number of particles in the gas remains constant.

The gas laws can be summarized and recalled by remembering the Ideal Gas Equation:

pV = nRT   =>   p = nRT/V   =>   p ∝ 1/V

This is a mathematical expression of Boyle's law.

pV = nRT   =>   pV = nRT   =>   V ∝ T

This is a mathematical expression of Charles' law:

"*The volume of gas is directly proportional to the absolute temperature provided the pressure and the number of particles in the gas remains constant.*"

Either Charles' law or Boyle's law could easily be the basis of a question in the EmSAT exam - so both should be learned.

10. C

Potassium is the **most reactive** element in the offered list.

This question becomes easier to answer when you notice that the other answer options are all noble gases (*inert* gases) which are all very unreactive! Potassium is a Group 1A metal that has an unpaired outer electron as part of its electronic configuration. This unpaired electron makes potassium very reactive. Potassium usually reacts with another element by donating that electron to the other atom - so that the electron can form a more stable electron *pair*.

The inert gases have paired electrons in full atomic orbitals/subshells - making them stable and unreactive.

11. D

Caesium is the **most reactive** element in the list of answer options.

A good student should remember that the Group 1A elements are more reactive as the group is descended. Caesium is the lowest member of the group given as a possible answer option and is the correct choice.

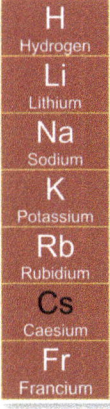

The lower the position of the atom in the Group 1A elements (alkali metals), the larger the atomic radius. So, the outer unpaired **s** subshell electron experiences a weaker attraction to the positive charge of the nucleus. Accordingly, this outer electron can more easily leave the atom as part of its chemical reaction with another atom.

Caesium reacts violently with water.

12. B

The concentration of the $HNO_{3(aq)}$ is **100 mM**.

The reaction between the acid and base is:

$KOH_{(aq)} + HNO_{3(aq)} \rightarrow H_2O_{(l)} + KNO_{3(aq)}$

This balanced reaction shows that equal amounts (*moles*) of potassium hydroxide and nitric acid must react together to produce water and potassium nitrate. So, for example, 50 ml of 50 mM KOH would require 50 ml of 50 mM HNO_3 for a complete reaction. However, the question stem indicates that only 25 ml of the HNO_3 was required to neutralize the base. This suggests that the nitric acid solution is *twice as strong* as the potassium hydroxide solution because only half as much volume of the nitric acid was needed. Accordingly, the nitric acid solution has a concentration of **2 x 50 mM => 100 mM**.

Another way to answer this question is to calculate the number of moles of KOH in the 50 ml of 50 mM solution - this number of moles *must equal the number of moles* in the 25 ml of HNO_3:

Moles of KOH in 50 ml of 50 mM solution => $(50/1000) \times 50 \times 10^{-3}$ = 2.5 millimoles
Moles of HNO_3 in 25 ml of *unknown* concentration = 2.5 millimoles
So, the concentration of $HNO_{3(aq)}$ is 2.5 millimoles in 25 ml = 100 millimoles in 1000 ml => **100 mM**

> For the EmSAT exam it is important to be able to balance chemical equations and carry out simple mole/molar calculations.

13. D

Liquids have definite volumes but **not a definite shape** - they shape themselves to the container.

Characteristics	State of matter
The matter has a definite volume and a definite shape.	SOLID
The matter has a definite volume but not a definite shape.	LIQUID
This matter has no definite shape nor a definite volume.	GAS

14. B

By convention equilibrium constants are always expressed as **product concentration**(s) divided by **reactant concentration**(s):

$$K_{eq} = [B]/[A] \qquad A_{(aq)} \rightleftharpoons B_{(aq)}$$

It is important to remember this rule. If the direction of the reaction is reversed then the concentrations in the equilibrium constants are inverted. So, the equilibrium constant would then be expressed as $K_{eq} = [A]/[B]$.

15. **A**
The question stem is describing a **solution** - these are **clear liquids** that contain **well dissolved** solutes that can pass unchanged through filter paper.
A comparison of the properties of solutions, suspensions and colloids are shown in the adjacent table. Obviously, they are not solids!

	Solutions	Suspensions	Colloids
Appearance	Clear	Cloudy	Cloudy
Consistency	Uniform and constant throughout.	Not uniform and separates/settles on standing.	Uniform and constant throughout.
Particle size	Less than 1 nm in diameter.	More than 100 nm in diameter.	1 - 100 nm in diameter.
Filtration	Cannot be separated by filtration.	Can be separated by filtration.	Cannot be separated by filtration.
Examples	Saline/salt water	Salad dressing	Milk

16. **B**
Liquid mixtures can be separated by distillation because of their **different boiling points** (using fractional distillation or simple distillation techniques).

Because the components of the mixture boil and hence evaporate at different temperatures, the different liquids can be collected by condensation separately.

17. **C**
The correct answer is **29.22** g of sodium chloride.

By definition a 1 molar solution (1 M) contains 1 mole of substance in 1 litre of liquid. The question stem informs the reader that 1 mole of sodium chloride has a mass of 58.44 g.

=> 1 litre of 1 M sodium chloride would require 58.44 g.
=> 0.5 litre of 1 M sodium chloride would require 0.5 x 58.44 g = **29.22** g

18. **A**
Isotopes are atoms of the same element that have nuclei with **different numbers of neutrons**.

Because the electron numbers/configurations are the same in the different isotopes, *the isotopes have the same chemical properties*. The physical properties of isotopes can vary because of the different mass of the nucleus. A classical example is normal water H_2O compared with heavy water D_2O. D = Deuterium, a heavier isotope of hydrogen whose nucleus contains a neutron. Accordingly, heavy water has a higher boiling point than normal water; 101.4 ºC versus 100 ºC.

19. **A**
The mass number minus the atomic number gives the **number of neutrons** in the nucleus.

The definition of **mass number** is the total number of protons and neutrons in a nucleus. The **atomic number** is the number of protons in the nucleus. So, subtracting the atomic number from the mass number will give the number of neutrons in the nucleus.

20. **D**
A **joule** is the SI (Système International) unit of **energy**.

The SI unit of pressure is pascal or N/m², the SI unit of mass is kilogram, kg, and the SI unit of volume is cubic metre, m³.

Students should ensure that they know the common SI units before taking the EmSAT chemistry exam.

21. C
Deposition is the process of transformation of a **gas to a solid**.

The process of transforming from a liquid to a solid is called freezing. The process of transforming from a solid to a gas is called sublimation. The process of transforming from a liquid to a gas is called boiling.

22. D
Metals are characteristically **good conductors** of electricity because of their metallic bonds.
The characteristic physical properties of metals are *malleability*, good *heat conduction* and good *electrical conduction*. The metallic bond is caused by a sea of delocalized electrons that hold together the metallic cations. These electrons are important in the good electrical conduction, heat conduction and malleability.

***Positively** charged metal ions in a sea of negatively charged electrons. This is the metallic bond.*

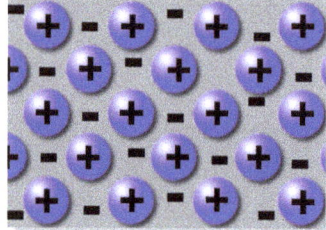

23. C
The element described is the alkali metal called **sodium**.

In contrast chlorine is a gas (a halogen) and neon is also a gas (a noble gas). Iron is a metal that is not very reactive and is not stored under oil.

24. B
In the periodic table elements are listed in the sequence of their **atomic numbers**.

The elements are not listed in the sequence of their mass numbers. Both metals and non-metals are shown in the periodic table.

25. A
At normal room temperature and pressure hydrogen is a **gas**.

Students revising for this exam should learn the normal physical states of the elements in the first two periods (rows) of the periodic table.

26. B
Exothermic reactions **produce heat**.

Endothermic reactions **absorb heat**. The words *endocaloric* and *exocaloric* do not exist.

27. A
Of the subatomic particles listed the **electron** has the **smallest mass**.

The proton has a mass of one atomic mass unit, the neutron has a mass of one atomic mass unit and the alpha particle has a mass of four atomic mass units (two protons and two neutrons).

28. C
CH_3COOH is called ethanoic **acid** or acetic **acid** - a 1 M solution would be **acidic**.

A pH below 7 is acidic. A pH above 7 is basic (alkaline).

29. C
This is an example of a **double displacement** reaction:

$$NaCl_{(aq)} + AgNO_{3(aq)} \longrightarrow NaNO_{3(aq)} + AgCl_{(s)}$$

The sodium chloride exchanges chloride for nitrate to become sodium nitrate, whereas at the same time the silver nitrate exchanges the nitrate for chloride to become silver chloride. Therefore this is double displacement reaction. This exam question could also have asked about *single displacement*, *synthesis*, *decomposition* or *combustion* reactions and these would be good reactions to revise for the exam.

30. D
The C-14 in the ancient wood must have decayed through two half-lives - **11,400** years.

It is reasonable to assume that when first made the wooden weapon had the same C-14 content as new modern wood. So, the ancient wooden weapon started with 100% C-14 content, dropped to 50% C-14 after 5,700 years and 25% C-14 after a further 5,700 years. The total number of years that must have passed is 11,400 years.

The key to understanding and answering this question correctly is remembering that a radioactive half-life is the time that it takes for half the original number of radioactive nuclides to disintegrate or decay.

31. A
The atomic mass an element is the **weighted average** of the masses of its isotopes.

The weighted average means the average real mass of the element - taking into account relative proportions of the element's isotopes in nature. For example, considering the isotopes of carbon:

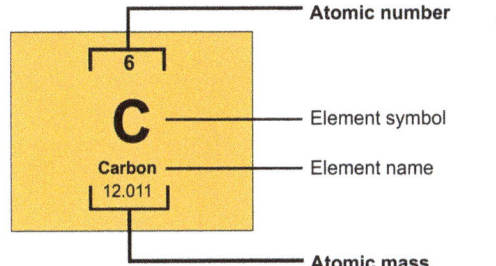

	Carbon-12	Carbon-13	Carbon-14
	Stable	Stable	Radioactive
Protons (= atomic number)	6	6	6
Neutrons	6	7	8
Abundance	98.93%	1.07%	trace

Proportion of each isotope in nature.

The Carbon-12 isotope makes the biggest contribution to the atomic mass which is why the atomic mass is almost 12. The reason why the atomic mass is actually greater than 12 is because more than 1% of natural carbon is the isotope Carbon-13.

32. A
The periodic table's **Group VIIIA** elements are **Noble gases**.

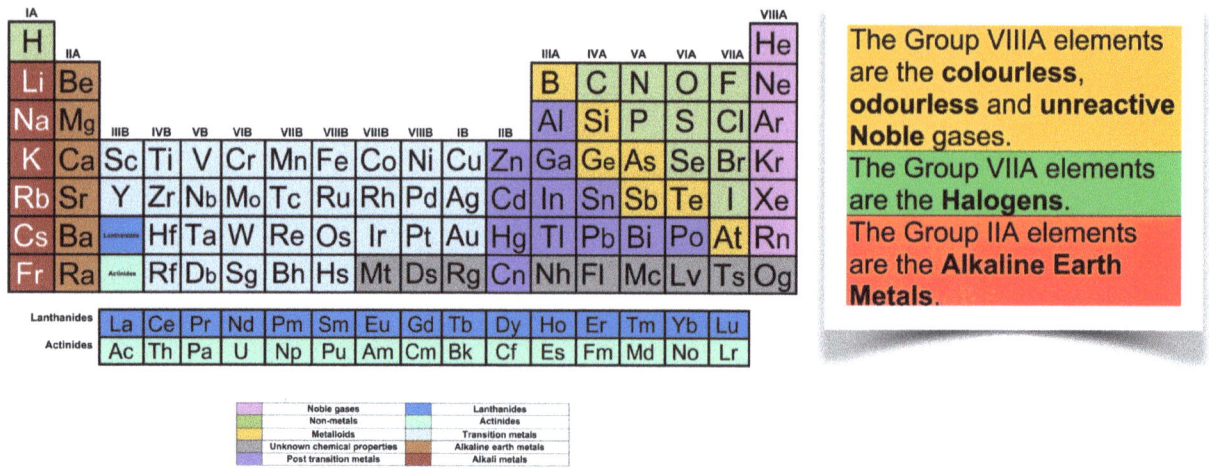

33. B
One of the properties of *solid iodine crystals* is that on heating **sublimation** to *iodine gas* occurs.

Another example of the sublimation process is solid carbon dioxide transforming directly to a gas. Solid carbon dioxide is also called ***dry ice*** and is used in films and in concerts to create misty fumes.

34. B
The physical properties of metals include **good conduction of heat** and electricity. Copper is the only answer option that is a metal.

The other answer options are non-metals or gases. *These are not good conductors of heat.*

35. C
As magnesium chloride is an ionic compound it does **not contain covalent bonds**.

A useful rule for identifying *ionic compounds* is that they occur when **non-metals** form compounds with **metals**. High melting points and electrical conductivity are characteristics of ionic compounds:

	Ionic	Molecular / Covalent
Composition	Composed of ions - occurs when metals and non-metals form compounds.	Occurs when non-metals form compounds.
Electrical Conductivity	Good electrical conductors when in liquid form/molten.	Poor conductors when in liquid form.
Melting Point	Usually higher than 300°C.	Usually lower than 300°C
Conductivity in water	Good conductors when dissolved in water.	Poor conductors in water (often do not dissolve in water).
Type of bond	Bonds formed by transfer of valence electrons.	Sharing of valence electrons.

36. B
The calcium in calcium chloride is in the form of **Ca^{2+}**.

Calcium is one of the alkaline earth metals (Group IIA) and in ionic form these metals have a +2 valency.

> It is important to know the common valences of each of the major groups of the periodic table.

37. B
OH⁻ is the chemical formula for *hydroxide* ion.

Ammonium	Acetate	Peroxide
NH_4^+	CH_3COO^-	O_2^{2-}

38. A
An alloy is a **mixture of metals** - it is a physical mixture.

Examples of alloys include:

Brass = copper and zinc.
Bronze = copper and tin.
Pewter = tin, copper, antimony and bismuth.
Solder = tin and lead.

Compounds are elements that have undergone a chemical reaction - so they are not physical mixtures.

39. B
A mole of chlorobenzene (C_6H_5Cl) will contain **6.02×10^{23}** molecules of chlorobenzene.

A mole of a substance contains the Avogadro constant number of those particles. The Avogadro constant is 6.02×10^{23} particles. 6.02×10^{22} is not the Avogadro constant!

40. C
Sn^{2+} is oxidized in the reaction.

The tin ion is oxidized from the +2 valency to the +4 valency. The tin ion has lost two electrons during the reaction - this **loss of electrons amounts to oxidation**.

$$HgCl_{2(aq)} + Sn^{2+}_{(aq)} \longrightarrow Sn^{4+}_{(aq)} + Hg_2Cl_{2(s)} + Cl^-_{(aq)}$$

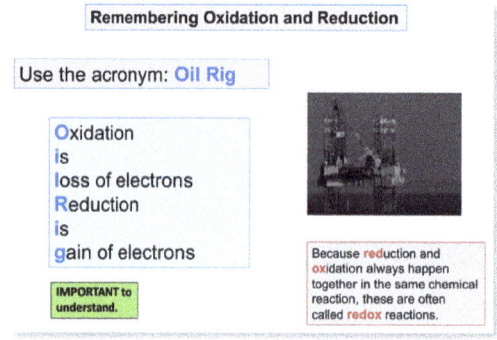

41. D
Dalton's Atomic Theory states that the **atom** is the smallest unit of matter.

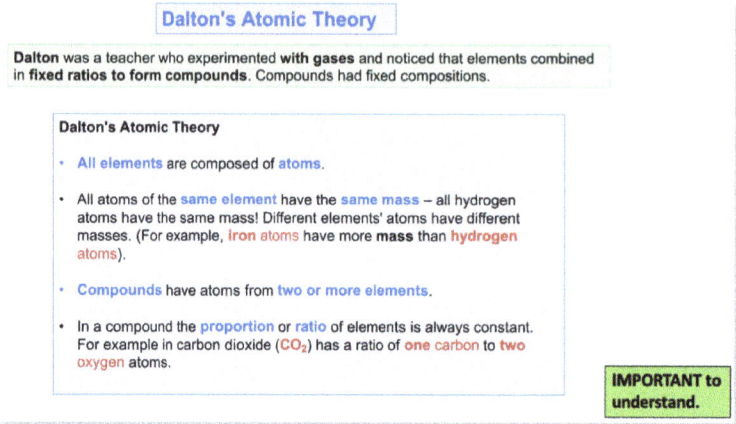

According to Dalton's theory the atom was considered to be an **indivisible and indestructible** component of matter. In addition, atoms of different elements had different masses. Finally, atoms in compounds exist in fixed proportions of the elements.

42. D
Chemical equilibria can be reached by approaching from the **product or reactant directions**.

By definition at equilibrium the forward and backward reaction rates are the same so the concentrations of reactants and products remain constant. At any specific temperature and pressure mixing the reactants or products together will reach the same equilibrium. So, chemical equilibria are not only reached by starting with substances on the reactant side of the equation:

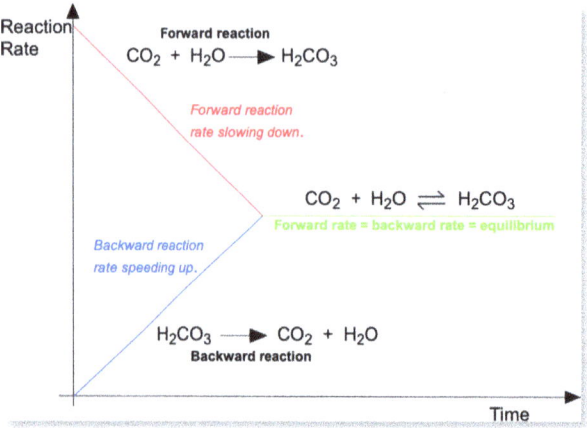

EmSAT Chemistry Achieve   Dr Sinclair Steele

43. B
Beryllium is a **Group IIA** alkaline earth metal:

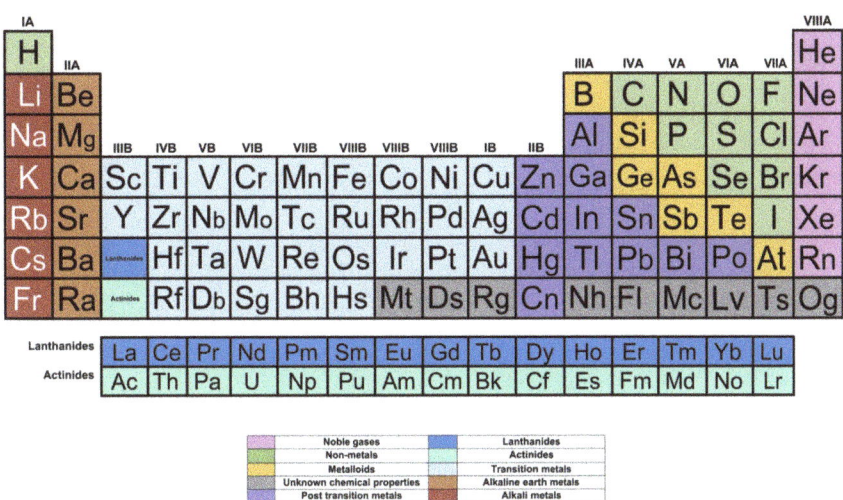

44. D
The correctly balanced equation is: $2C_2H_6 + 7O_2 \Rightarrow 4CO_2 + 6H_2O$

A balanced equation means that the number of atoms of each element are the same on the left and right of the equation. Because of the **seven** oxygen molecules there are **14** oxygen atoms as reactants and **14** oxygen atoms in the products. Similarly, the reactants have **four** carbon atoms and the products have **four** carbon atoms. Similarly, there are **12** hydrogen atoms in the reactants and products respectively.

Students are advised to practise balancing equations like this for the EmSAT exam.

45. A
The **products** with the **least enthalpy** compared with the reactants will release the most energy.

The biggest drop in enthalpy occurs in **A** where the energy of **P** (products) is much less than **R** (reactants). The energy difference is released as heat - so this is an exothermic reaction. The reverse is true for **D** and so that is an endothermic reaction.

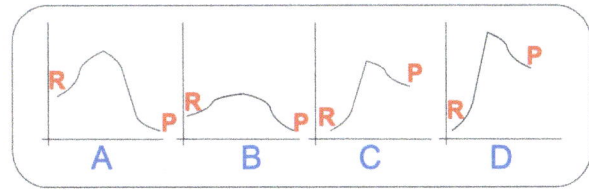

46. D
PV=nRT is the ideal gas equation.

P = pressure of the gas
V = volume of the gas

n = number of moles of the gas
R = universal/ideal gas constant
T = temperature of the gas (in Kelvin)

47. C
The maximum possible number of electrons in the *p* subshell of an atom is **6**.

Be aware of the following as part of your revision programme:
s subshell => maximum of two electrons
p subshell => maximum of six electrons
d subshell => maximum of ten electrons
f subshell => maximum of fourteen electrons

48. A
The correct equilibrium constant is $K_{eq} = [H_2O]^2 \times [Cl_2] / [HCl]^4 \times [O_2]$.

The general expression for describing equilibrium constants is shown:

Equilibrium Constant

For a general reversible reaction such as:

$$aA + bB \rightleftharpoons cC + dD$$

The equilibrium constant K_{eq} is expressed:

$$K_{eq} = \frac{[C]^c[D]^d}{[A]^a[B]^b} \qquad [\ ] = \text{concentration}$$

49. D
The chemical combination of two elements to form a single compound is termed **synthesis**.

The major chemical reaction types are summarized in the adjacent diagram.

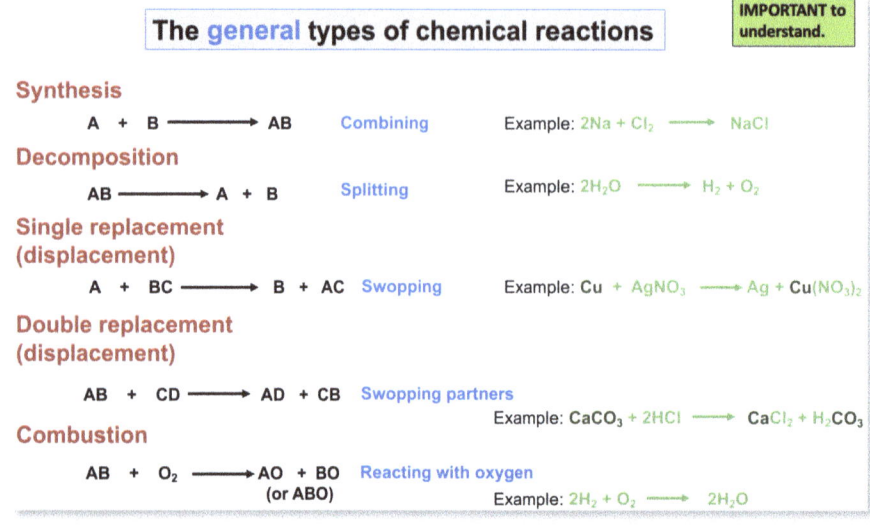

50. **C**
A molecule is polyatomic, composed of covalently bonded atoms and may be water soluble but is **not charged**.

Ions can be polyatomic or mono-atomic but they are **always charged**.

Test Two

1. Which of the following is a strong acid?

○ A. Aqueous sodium hydroxide solution
○ B. Aqueous ethanoic acid solution
○ C. Aqueous hydrochloric acid solution
○ D. Aqueous ammonia solution

2. Silicon has an atomic number of 14 and its electronic configuration is $1s^22s^22p^63s^23p^2$. Carbon has an atomic number of 6. What is carbon's electronic configuration?

○ A. $1s^22s^22p^63s^2$
○ B. $1s^22s^22p^63s^23p^4$
○ C. $1s^22s^22p^2$
○ D. $1s^22s^2$

3. Which of the following is not true of a chemical equilibrium?

○ A. The equilibrium constant is calculated by dividing the product concentration by the reactant concentration.
○ B. The forward reaction rate equals the backward reaction rate.
○ C. The quantity of products is constant at equilibrium.
○ D. The equilibrium does not depend on temperature or pressure.

4.

$$N_2 + 3H_2 \overset{\text{Exothermic}}{\underset{\text{Endothermic}}{\rightleftharpoons}} 2NH_3$$

For the equilibrium above, what would happen if you increased the quantity of NH_3?

○ A. The reaction equilibrium would move to the right.
○ B. The reaction equilibrium would move to the left.
○ C. The reaction equilibrium would not change.
○ D. The quantity of H_2 would decrease.

5. If you increase the temperature of a gas then you:

○ A. Increase the kinetic energy of its molecules.
○ B. Decrease the kinetic energy of its molecules.
○ C. Always increase its volume.
○ D. Always decrease its volume.

6. In Rutherford's Gold Foil Experiment why were some alpha particles deflected/reflected back?

- A. Because the nucleus was positively charged and its mass was in the centre of the atom.
- B. Because the nucleus was very big.
- C. Because the nucleus was negatively charged.
- D. Because of the Plum Pudding Model.

7. Which of the following solutions of sodium chloride at 25°C contains the most of this ionic solute?

- A. An unsaturated solution.
- B. A saturated solution.
- C. A supersaturated solution.
- D. Pure water.

8. What is the mass of a proton?

- A. 0 atomic mass units
- B. 1 atomic mass unit
- C. 2 atomic mass units
- D. 3 atomic mass units

9. A saturated hydrocarbon compound has carbon atom to carbon atom:

- A. Triple covalent bonds
- B. Double covalent bonds
- C. Single covalent bonds
- D. Ionic bonds

10. The reversible physical change that occurs when a substance changes from one state of matter to another is called:

- A. Phase change
- B. Heat of vaporization
- C. Heat of fusion
- D. Plasma

11. Which of the following statements about solubility is true?

- A. Butter dissolves well in water.
- B. Magnesium chloride dissolves well in water.
- C. Gases dissolve more in water as the temperature increases.
- D. Polar substances dissolve well in nonpolar solvents.

12. Which of the following reactions shows the oxidation of Ti²⁺?

- A. Ti => Ti²⁺ + 2e⁻
- B. Ti³⁺ + e⁻ => Ti²⁺
- C. Ti²⁺ + 2e⁻ => Ti
- D. Ti²⁺ => Ti³⁺ + e⁻

13. Which of the following is a property of a basic solution?

- A. Turns litmus paper red.
- B. Tastes sour.
- C. Neutralizes sodium hydroxide.
- D. Makes the skin of the fingers feel slippery.

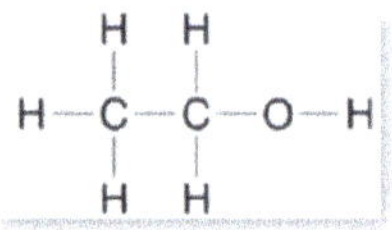

$$H-\underset{\underset{H}{|}}{\overset{\overset{H}{|}}{C}}-\underset{\underset{H}{|}}{\overset{\overset{H}{|}}{C}}-O-H$$

14. What kind of compound is shown above?

- A. Halocarbon
- B. Ester
- C. Alcohol
- D. Carboxylic acid

15. Which of the following is true about acids?

- A. An acid has a pH greater than 7.
- B. An acid has a pH of 7.
- C. An acid has a pH less than 7.
- D. Acid is usually present in bleach.

16. Calculate the mass percentage of Ba in this compound: **BaSO₄**.
(Atomic masses: Ba = 137, S = 32, O = 16)

- A. 39%
- B. 49%
- C. 59%
- D. 69%

17. Considering the nuclear reaction below in which X represents the nuclide product:

$$^{235}_{92}U + \ ^{4}_{2}He \Rightarrow X$$

Which of the answer options is the nuclide **X**?

- A. $^{239}_{92}U$
- B. $^{231}_{94}Pu$
- C. $^{239}_{93}Np$
- D. $^{239}_{94}Pu$

18. What is the total number of electrons shared in the bond between the carbon and nitrogen atoms in the following molecule?

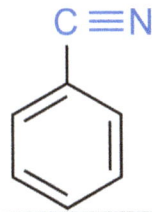

- A. 2
- B. 4
- C. 6
- D. 8

19. Which of the following elements has chemical properties most similar to sodium?

- A. Chlorine
- B. Potassium
- C. Iron
- D. Aluminium

20. A student has conducted a titration by adding 10 ml of an unknown concentration of $KOH_{(aq)}$ to 10 ml of 1 M $H_2SO_{4(aq)}$. What is the molar concentration of $KOH_{(aq)}$?

- A. 1
- B. 2
- C. 3
- D. 4

21. Which of the following equations represents condensation?

- A. $H_2O_{(l)} => H_2O_{(g)}$
- B. $H_2O_{(g)} => H_2O_{(l)}$
- C. $H_2O_{(s)} => H_2O_{(l)}$
- D. $H_2O_{(l)} => H_2O_{(s)}$

22. The molecular formula of glucose is $C_6H_{12}O_6$. What is the empirical formula of glucose?

- A. CH_2O
- B. $C_2H_4O_2$
- C. CO_2
- D. CH_2

23. Which of the following reactions shows the reduction of O^-?

- A. $O \Rightarrow O^{2+} + 2e^-$
- B. $O^- \Rightarrow O + e^-$
- C. $O^- + e^- \Rightarrow O^{2-}$
- D. $O^{2-} \Rightarrow O^- + e^-$

24. Calculate the mass percentage of *carbon* in this compound: $CHCl_3$.
(Atomic masses: C = 12, H = 1, Cl = 35.5)

- A. 10%
- B. 20%
- C. 30%
- D. 40%

25. "The volume of an ideal gas at constant pressure is directly proportional to the absolute temperature, if the number of gas particles is constant." This is a statement of:

- A. Boyle's law
- B. Charles' law
- C. Newton's law
- D. Faraday's law

26. The adjacent reaction is an example of what type of chemical reaction?

$$2Al_2O_{3(s)} \Rightarrow 4Al_{(s)} + 3O_{2(g)}$$

- A. direct combination / synthesis reaction.
- B. single displacement reaction.
- C. double displacement reaction.
- D. decomposition reaction.

27. Which of the following is the description of a gas?

- A. The opposite state of matter to a plasma.
- B. The state of matter in which a material has neither a definite shape nor a definite volume.

○ C. The state of matter in which a material has a definite volume and a definite shape.
○ D. The state of matter in which a material has a definite volume but not a definite shape.

28. What kind of bonding is responsible for water being a liquid at room temperature and pressure?

○ A. Hydrogen bonds
○ B. London forces
○ C. Ionic bonds
○ D. Covalent bonds

29. The anion S^{2-} is called:

○ A. Sulphide or Sulfide
○ B. Sulphate or Sulfate
○ C. Sulphite or Sulfite
○ D. Sulphuric or Sulfuric

30. Which equation is correctly balanced?

○ A. $Na + Br_2 \Rightarrow 2NaBr$
○ B. $C_2H_6 + 3O_2 \Rightarrow 2CO_2 + H_2O$
○ C. $2NaOH + H_2SO_4 \Rightarrow 2H_2O + Na_2SO_4$
○ D. $2C + O_2 \Rightarrow CO_2$

31. Which of the following statements is not true?

○ A. A mole of any ideal gas occupies approximately 22.4 L at standard temperature and pressure (0 °C and 1 atm).
○ B. For an ideal gas PV=nRT.
○ C. Increasing the temperature of a gas increases the kinetic energy of its molecules.
○ D. H_2 is not a gas at room temperature and pressure.

32. Considering the reaction: $H_2SO_{4(aq)} + Zn_{(s)} \Rightarrow ZnSO_{4(aq)} + H_{2(g)}$
Why is the reaction faster when powdered zinc rather than a lump of zinc of the same mass, is used?

○ A. There is a greater concentration of powdered zinc.
○ B. Powdered zinc has a relatively larger surface area.
○ C. The single piece of zinc is more reactive.
○ D. More heat energy is generated by the powdered zinc.

33. If a catalyst is added to the reaction below *at equilibrium* which of the statements is true?

- A. The concentration of reactants increases.
- B. The concentration of reactants decreases.
- C. The concentration of reactants remains the same.
- D. None of the above.

34. Which one of the following polymers is synthetic?

- A. Protein
- B. Nylon
- C. Cellulose
- D. DNA

35. What units can be used to describe the energy released during a chemical reaction?

- A. mmHg or pascal
- B. joule or calorie
- C. amp or ampere
- D. celsius or kelvin

36. A straight chain alkane with three carbon atoms is called:

- A. Methane
- B. Propane
- C. Pentane
- D. Heptane

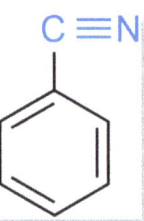

37. What kind of compound is shown above?

- A. Alkane
- B. Amide
- C. Ether
- D. Cyanide

38. An elevator containing 350 kg of people goes up five floors (50 m) and stops. The elevator has gained:

- A. Chemical energy
- B. Potential energy
- C. Electrical energy
- D. Kinetic energy

39. Which two elements have the most similar chemical properties?

- A. Plutonium and Iron
- B. Carbon and Fluorine
- C. Neon and Argon
- D. Aluminium and Sodium

40. The forces of attraction that exist between nonpolar molecules, such as benzene, are called:

- A. London forces
- B. Hydrogen bonds
- C. Covalent bonds
- D. Ionic forces

41. What is the chemical formula of aluminium sulphate?

- A. $Al_2(SO_4)_3$
- B. $AlSO_4$
- C. Al_2SO_4
- D. $Al(SO_4)_3$

42. A hydrocarbon has the empirical formula CH_2. Which of the following compounds could be this hydrocarbon?

- A. CH_4
- B. C_2H_6
- C. $C_6H_{12}O_6$
- D. C_4H_8

43. The molecular mass of magnesium chloride is 95 g/mol. 190 grams of $MgCl_2$ are dissolved in water to make a 1000 ml solution. What is the molarity of the $MgCl_2$ solution?

- A. 0.5 M
- B. 1 M
- C. 2 M
- D. 4 M

44. When HNO$_3$(aq) reacts with KOH(aq) the products are:

○ A. A salt and water
○ B. A salt and hydrogen gas
○ C. An acid and a base
○ D. An ester and water

45. Which of the following is not an allotrope of carbon?

○ A. Graphite
○ B. Diamond
○ C. Buckminsterfullerene
○ D. Lead

$$^{235}_{92}U + {}^{0}_{1}n \longrightarrow {}^{236}_{92}U \longrightarrow {}^{141}_{36}Ba + {}^{92}_{36}Kr + 3\,{}^{1}_{0}n$$

46. The nuclear reaction that occurs in a nuclear power station is described above.

Which of the following statements about this reaction is true?

○ A. Fission of the uranium atom occurs.
○ B. Fusion of the uranium atom occurs.
○ C. Three free protons are produced by the nuclear reaction.
○ D. No heat energy is released during the reaction.

47. A natural polymer that contains nitrogen and is present in large amounts in meat and hair is most likely to be:

○ A. Cellulose
○ B. Protein
○ C. Starch
○ D. Nylon

48. The molecular mass of ethanoic acid is 60 g/mol. How much ethanoic acid must be dissolved in a final volume of 500 ml in order to produce a 1.5 M solution of aqueous ethanoic acid?

○ A. 15 g
○ B. 30 g
○ C. 45 g
○ D. 60 g

49. Which material can be decomposed?

- A. iron
- B. iodine
- C. methane
- D. germanium

50. What is the mass of the beta particle?

- A. One atomic mass unit.
- B. The same as an electron.
- C. Two atomic mass units.
- D. The same as an alpha particle.

TEST TWO

ANSWER SECTION

Test Two - Answer Key									
1)	C	11)	B	21)	B	31)	D	41)	A
2)	C	12)	D	22)	A	32)	B	42)	D
3)	D	13)	D	23)	C	33)	C	43)	C
4)	B	14)	C	24)	A	34)	B	44)	A
5)	A	15)	C	25)	B	35)	B	45)	D
6)	A	16)	C	26)	D	36)	B	46)	A
7)	C	17)	D	27)	B	37)	D	47)	B
8)	B	18)	C	28)	A	38)	B	48)	C
9)	C	19)	B	29)	A	39)	C	49)	C
10)	A	20)	B	30)	C	40)	A	50)	B

1. C
Aqueous hydrochloric acid solution is a **strong** acid.

A strong acid is almost completely ionized (separated into respective anions -ve and cations +ve) in water. So, hydrochloric acid becomes $H^+_{(aq)}$ and $Cl^-_{(aq)}$ in water. $HCl_{(g)} + H2O_{(l)} \rightarrow H^+_{(aq)} + Cl^-_{(aq)}$

In contrast, a weak acid like ethanoic acid is **only partly ionized** in water - a large proportion of the ethanoic acid remains as the molecule. An equilibrium is formed that favours the ethanoic acid molecule:
$CH_3COOH_{(l)} + H_2O \leftrightarrows CH_3COO^-_{(aq)} + H^+_{(aq)}$

Aqueous sodium hydroxide is a strong base because it almost completely dissociates into $Na^+_{(aq)}$ and $OH^-_{(aq)}$. Aqueous ammonia is a weak base because most of the ammonia remains as a molecule:

$NH_{3(aq)} + H_2O_{(l)} \leftrightarrows NH^{4+}_{(aq)} + OH^-_{(aq)}$

2. C
Carbon's electronic configuration is **$1s^2 2s^2 2p^2$**.

Magnesium's electronic configuration is $1s^2 2s^2 2p^6 3s^2$.
Sulphur's electronic configuration is $1s^2 2s^2 2p^6 3s^2 3p^4$.
Beryllium's electronic configuration is $1s^2 2s^2$.

3. D
A chemical equilibrium is usually affected by **temperature** or **pressure**.

Chemical equilibria that include endothermic or exothermic reactions are affected by temperature. The equilibria follow **Le Chatelier's principle and move to decrease the perturbation (absorb or emit heat)**. Similarly, gaseous reactions that have unequal numbers of molecules in the balanced equation are affected by pressure:

4. B
If the quantity of ammonia molecules is increased then the **equilibrium will move to the left** - more hydrogen molecules and nitrogen molecules will be formed.

If the quantity of nitrogen or hydrogen molecules is increased then equilibrium will move to the right - more ammonia molecules will be formed.

5. A

If you **increase the temperature** of a gas you **increase the kinetic energy** of its molecules. This is because the average kinetic energy of gas molecules is directly proportional to the absolute temperature. The absolute temperature scales are Kelvin and Rankine.

> The four major temperature scales are Celsius, Fahrenheit, **Kelvin** and **Rankine.** Kelvin and Rankine are the absolute temperature scales.

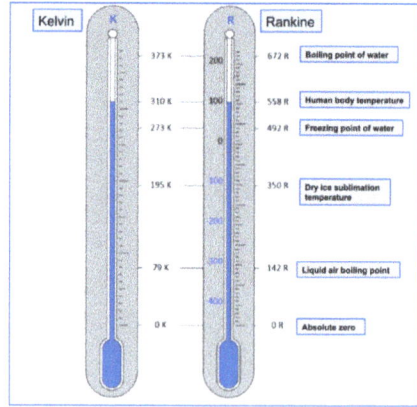

6. A

The alpha particles were **reflected** back because the atomic mass and total positive charge were concentrated in the **centre of the target nuclei**.

The nucleus is positively charged not negatively charged. The **nucleus** takes up a very small proportion of the total volume of the atom and so **is very small**. The *Plum Pudding Model* is **Thomson's** view of the atom and does not have a nucleus - if this view had been completely accurate then alpha particles would not be reflected or significantly deflected.

In Rutherford's experiment small heavy alpha particles were fired at and hit denser and heavier nuclei that were positively charged. This collision caused the deflections and reflections.

7. C

A supersaturated solution **contains more solute** than the maximum (stable) solubility at that temperature.

A *saturated* solution has enough dissolved solute to **reach the maximum solubility** at the temperature of interest. An *unsaturated* solution has **less dissolved solute** than the maximum solubility at the temperature of interest.

8. B

The mass of a proton is **1 atomic mass unit**.

One atomic unit is equal to one twelfth (1/12) of the mass of the most common isotope of carbon, Carbon-12.

Atomic Mass Unit: $1 \text{ u} = 1.66 \times 10^{-27}$ kg

Common Atomic Masses:
○ Proton = 1.007276 u
○ Neutron = 1.008665 u
● Electron = 0.00055 u
Hydrogen 1.007825 u

9. C

A saturated hydrocarbon compound has **single covalent carbon to carbon** bonds (C-C).

Unsaturated hydrocarbon compounds have at least one **double bond** or one **triple bond** between adjacent carbon atoms (C=C or C≡C). Ionic bonds are not classed as saturated or unsaturated.

10. A

The reversible physical change that occurs when a substance changes from one state of matter to another is called a **phase change**.

The **heat of vaporization** is defined as the amount of **heat** energy needed to turn 1 g of a liquid into a vapor, without a rise in the temperature of the liquid. The heat of fusion is the quantity of heat energy necessary to change 1 g of a solid to a liquid with no temperature change. Plasma is the state of matter that is *an ionized gas with free electrons,* usually at very high temperatures.

11. B

Magnesium chloride dissolves well in water because it is an **ionic solute** dissolving in a **polar solvent**.

The magnesium ions form ion-dipole bonds with water to facilitate solvation and the chloride ions similarly also form **ion-dipole bonds**. The general rule is that *like dissolves like* - so polar solutes tend to dissolve in polar solvents and nonpolar solutes tend to dissolve in nonpolar solvents. Accordingly, butter does not dissolve well in water. Similarly, polar solutes do not dissolve well in nonpolar solvents (sodium chloride does not dissolve well in oil).

12. D

This reaction shows an **oxidation** process: $Ti^{2+} \Rightarrow Ti^{3+} + e^-$

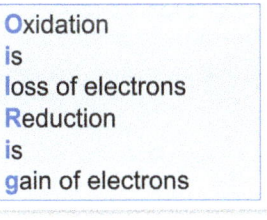

Reaction (A) $Ti \Rightarrow Ti^{2+} + 2e^-$ is also an oxidation reaction but it is **titanium metal** that is oxidized not the **titanium ion**. Reactions (B) and (C) are reduction reactions.

13. D

A basic solution is one that produces hydroxide ions in water and it feels **slippery** because of **saponification** of skin oils.

Saponification is the process of making soap - in this case it happens on the surface of the skin. This is a **base catalyzed hydrolysis** of esters to create a carboxylic acid salt that is a **simple soap**. A base turns litmus paper blue and an acid turns litmus paper red. **Acids taste sour** (but bases do not). A good way to remember this is to think of the sour taste of vinegar that is mainly acetic acid/ethanoic acid. A base cannot neutralize sodium hydroxide because sodium hydroxide is also a base - only an acid can neutralize sodium hydroxide.

14. C

The compound shown is an **alcohol**.

Below are examples of the structures of halocarbons, esters and carboxylic acids:

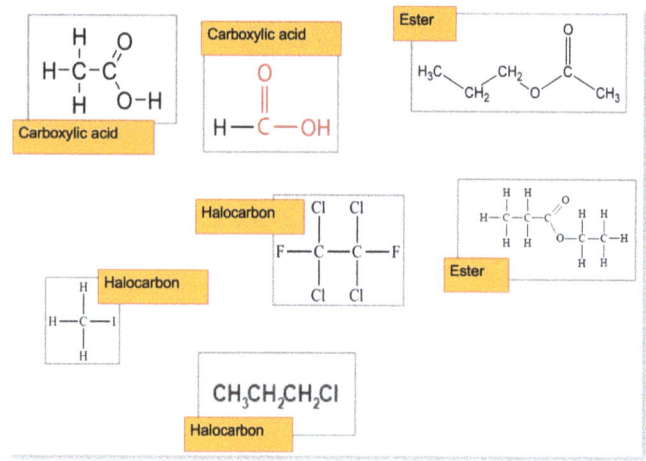

15. C
An acid has a pH **less than 7**.

A base has a pH greater than 7. Bleaches contain alkalis not acids.

16. C
The mass percentage of Ba in **BaSO₄** is **59%**.

It can be calculated:

(Atomic masses: Ba = 137, S = 32, O = 16)
Atomic mass of barium is **137**.
Formula mass/Molar mass of BaSO₄ is 137 + 32 + (16 x 4) = **233**
Mass percentage of Ba = 137/233 = **59%**

17. D
The nuclear reaction yields **plutonium-239.**

The element X can be deduced by adding 235 and 4 together to make 239 (mass number).

Then, adding 92 to 2 makes 94 (atomic number) => $^{239}_{94}Pu$

18. C
The -**CN** group is called **cyanide** and contains a triple covalent bond so **six electrons are shared**.

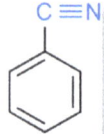

19. B
The element that has chemical properties most similar to **sodium is potassium** because they are both **Group IA** elements.

Chlorine is a halogen gas and so is chemically dissimilar from **sodium**. **Iron** is a transition metal that is relatively unreactive. Finally, **aluminium** is a Group IIIA metal that is trivalent compared with monovalent sodium.

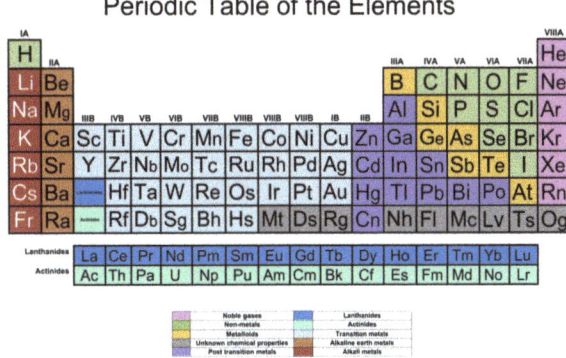

20. B
The **molar** concentration of $KOH_{(aq)}$ is **2 M**.

The balanced equation for the titration is given below:
$H_2SO_{4(aq)}$ + **2**$KOH_{(aq)}$ => $K_2SO_{4(aq)}$ + **2**$H_2O_{(l)}$
1   2   1   2

The balanced equation indicates that **one** part of sulphuric acid requires **two** parts of potassium hydroxide - or alternatively there must be twice as much potassium hydroxide as sulphuric acid for a completely titrated reaction. So, 1 M sulphuric acid **requires 2 M potassium hydroxide**.

21. B
B. $H_2O_{(g)}$ => $H_2O_{(l)}$ represents **condensation**.

The commonest daily example of condensation occurs when warm air flows onto a cold surface like a window or a cold bottle of water. The water in the air is initially in the form of a gas but changes state to a liquid when it comes into contact with the cold surface. This is **condensation**.

22. A
The empirical formula of glucose is **CH_2O**.

The empirical formula is the simplest basic ratio of elements in a compound. Examples are shown in the table:

Name of compound	Molecular formula	Empirical formula
Benzene	C_6H_6	CH
Butane	C_4H_{10}	C_2H_5
Hydrogen peroxide	H_2O_2	HO
Water	H_2O	H_2O
Dinitrogen tetroxide	N_2O_4	NO_2
Ethyne	C_2H_2	CH
Ethanol	C_2H_6O	C_2H_6O

23. C

This reaction O⁻ + e⁻ => O²⁻ shows the O⁻ gaining an electron and this is **reduction**.

A. O => O²⁺ + 2e⁻   Oxidation reaction
B. O⁻ => O + e⁻   Oxidation reaction
D. O²⁻ => O⁻ + e⁻   Oxidation reaction

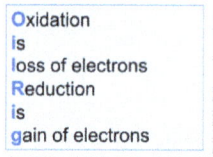

24. A

The mass percentage of C in **CHCl₃** is 10%.

It can be calculated:

(Atomic masses: C = 12, H = 1, Cl = 35.5)
Atomic mass of carbon is **12**.
Molecular Mass of **CHCl₃** is 12 + 1 + (35.5 x 3) = **119.5**
Mass percentage of C = 12/119.5 = **10%**

25. B

The question stem is a **statement of Charles' law**.

Newton's laws relate to the physics of motion. Faraday's law relates to electric charge/magnetic field. Boyle's law states that the pressure of a given mass of an ideal gas is inversely proportional to its volume at a constant temperature.

26. D

2Al₂O₃(s) => 4Al(s) + 3O₂(g)   This is a decomposition reaction.

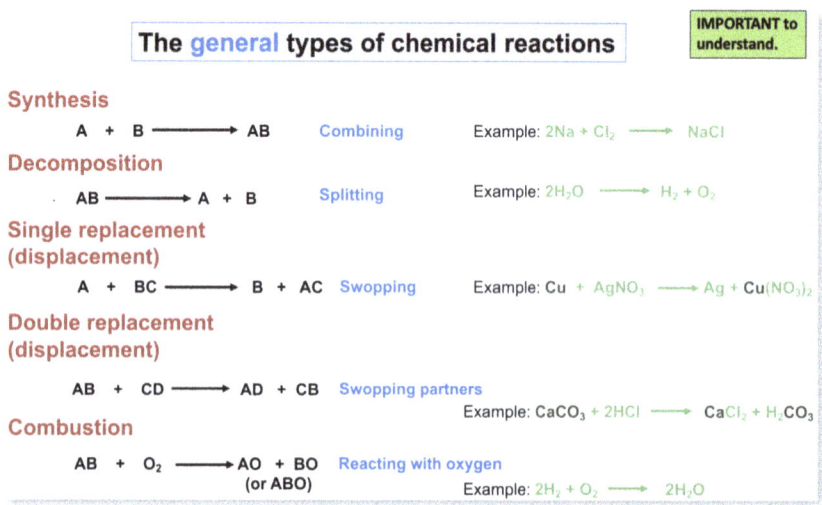

27. B

Gases have neither definite volumes **nor definite shapes** - they shape themselves to the container.

Characteristics	State of matter
The matter has a **definite volume** and a **definite shape**.	SOLID
The matter has **a definite volume** but **not a definite shape**.	LIQUID
This matter has **no definite shape nor a definite volume**.	GAS

28. A
Hydrogen bonds are responsible for water being a liquid at room temperature and pressure.

The intermolecular forces between water molecules are hydrogen bonds and are a form of **intermolecular dipole forces**. London forces are weak intermolecular forces that occur between uncharged nonpolar molecules. Ionic bonds are formed by electron transfer to form charged ions/ polyatomic ions that are attracted to each other. Covalent bonds are formed by shared electron pairs and are **intra**molecular forces not **inter**molecular forces.

29. A
The anion S^{2-} is called **sulphide** or **sulfide**.

Sulphate/Sulfate → SO_4^{2-}
Sulphite/Sulfite → SO_3^{2-}
Sulphuric/Sulfuric (acid) → H_2SO_4

30. C
This equation is correctly balanced: **2**$NaOH$ + H_2SO_4 => **2**H_2O + Na_2SO_4

Left side of the chemical equation: **2Na**   Right side of the chemical equation: **2Na**
                                                            4H   **4H**
                                                            6O   **6O**
                                                            1S   **1S**

The number of atoms of each type is the same on both sides of the chemical equation *so the chemical reaction is balanced*. The reactions below have now been balanced:

○ A. **2**Na + Br_2 => **2**$NaBr$
○ B. **2**C_2H_6 + **7**O_2 => **4**CO_2 + **6**H_2O
○ D. **2**C + **2**O_2 => **2**CO_2

31. D
H_2 (molecular hydrogen) is a **gas** at room temperature and pressure.

The other statements are all true:

A. A mole of any gas occupies 22.4 L at standard temperature and pressure (0 °C and 1 atm).
B. For an ideal gas PV=nRT.
C. Increasing the temperature of a gas increases the kinetic energy of its molecules.

32. B
Powdering the zinc increases the **surface area to volume ratio** of the solid and so there is more space for the reaction, making the chemical reaction faster.

Powdering the zinc does not increase the concentration of zinc, so this is not the explanation for the increased reaction rate. A single piece of zinc is not more reactive than multiple pieces of zinc. The reaction shown is not described as exothermic and so no more heat is generated by the powdered zinc.

$H_2SO_{4(aq)} + Zn_{(s)} \Rightarrow ZnSO_{4(aq)} + H_{2(g)}$

33. C
At **equilibrium** the concentration of **reactants and products** is constant - the addition of a catalyst does not change this.

A catayst increases the speed of the forward and back reactions by lowering the activation energy but does not change the equilibrium position - so the concentrations of reactants and products are also unchanged (or constant). A catalyst will speed up the arrival at equilibrium.

34. B
Nylon is a **synthetic polyamide polymer** made from carboxylic acids and amines.

The most well known use of nylon is in **synthetic clothing**. In contrast, protein, cellulose and DNA are natural polymers. Protein is essentially a poly amino acid that is a component of all human cells and all enzymes. **Muscle** (meat) contains a high proportion of **protein**. Cellulose is essentially a poly glucose and is present in plant cell walls. **Wood** contains a large amount of **cellulose**. DNA (deoxyribonucleic acid) is a polynucleotide and is the important component of human **genetic material**.

35. B
Joules and calories are units of **energy**.

Pascals and mmHg are units of **pressure**. *Amp* is short for ampere which is a unit of electric **current**. Celsius and kelvin are used to measure **temperature**.

36. B
A straight chain alkane with **three carbon** atoms is called **propane**.

Name of straight chain alkane		Number of carbon atoms
Methane	CH_4	One
Ethane	C_2H_6	Two
Propane	C_3H_8	Three
Butane	C_4H_{10}	Four
Pentane	C_5H_{12}	Five
Hexane	C_6H_{14}	Six
Heptane	C_7H_{16}	Seven
Octane	C_8H_{18}	Eight
Nonane	C_9H_{20}	Nine
Decane	$C_{10}H_{22}$	Ten

37. D
The **-CN** functional group is present in **cyanide** compounds.

The functional group for a (primary) amide is **-CONH$_2$**.
The functional group for ether is **-C-O-C-**.
Alkanes contain only **-C-H** functional groups.

38. B
The elevator raised 350 kg and so gained **potential energy**.

Potential energy is described as **PE = mgh**
$\qquad\qquad\qquad$ **P**otential energy = **m**ass x **g**ravity x **h**eight

The amount of potential energy gained is:
$\qquad\qquad\qquad$ **PE** = 350 x 10 x 50 = 175 kJ

39. C
Neon and argon are in the same group of the periodic table (noble gases) and so have similar chemical properties.

Iron is a transitional metal whereas plutonium is an actinide metal, so they do not have similar chemical properties. Fluorine is a halogen (Group VIIA) whereas carbon is a Group IVA element, so they do not have similar chemical properties. Sodium is an alkali metal (Group IA) whereas aluminium is a Group IIIA element and so these too are chemically dissimilar.

40. A
The forces of attraction that exist between **two nonpolar molecules**, such as benzene, are called **London** forces.

Even though benzene has no overall dipole, at any one moment its electron density may not be absolutely symmetrical, so resulting in a temporary dipole. This can cause a temporary dipole in a nearby molecule. The weak forces of attraction between these adjacent temporary dipoles in these uncharged molecules are called London forces.

41. A
The chemical formula for aluminium sulphate is Al$_2$(SO$_4$)$_3$.

The *aluminium* ion is **trivalent (+3)** and the *sulphate* ion is **divalent (-2)** - together they form the compound Al$_2$(SO$_4$)$_3$.

42. D
Only the hydrocarbon **C$_4$H$_8$** has the empirical formula CH$_2$.

CH$_4$ has the empirical formula **CH$_4$**.
C$_2$H$_6$ has the empirical formula **CH$_3$**.
C$_6$H$_{12}$O$_6$ has the empirical formula **CH$_2$O**.

43. C
The **molarity** of the magnesium chloride solution is **2 M**.

As the molecular mass of magnesium chloride is 95 g/mol, then one mole of magnesium chloride has a mass of 95 grams. So 190 grams of magnesium chloride is two moles.
Adding two moles in 1000 ml of liquid amounts to a **2 M solution of magnesium chloride**.

44. A
When $HNO_{3(aq)}$ reacts with $KOH_{(aq)}$ the products are $KNO_{3(aq)}$ and H_2O - these are the **salt** and **water**, respectively.

The above reaction is between an acid and a base reacting to form a salt and water.
A **metal** and an **acid** react to form a **salt** and **hydrogen gas**.
An **alcohol** and a **carboxylic acid** react to form an **ester** and **water**.
A smart student would be wise to memorize these three chemical reaction patterns!

45. D
Lead (Pb) is not an allotrope of carbon.

Graphite, diamond and buckminsterfullerene are allotropes of carbon. The structures of each allotrope directly relate to their physical properties.

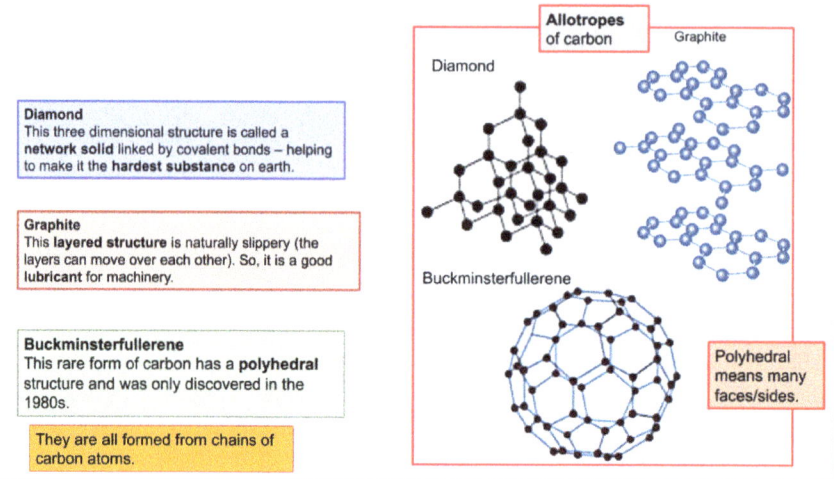

46. A
The reaction shows uranium *breaking* into barium and krypton - this is a **fission** reaction.

$$^{235}_{92}U + ^{0}_{1}n \longrightarrow ^{236}_{92}U \longrightarrow ^{141}_{36}Ba + ^{92}_{36}Kr + 3\,^{1}_{0}n$$

A fusion reaction would involve two nuclei becoming one nucleus - this is not occurring in the above reaction. Also, this reaction releases three neutrons not three protons. The usefulness of the **nuclear reaction** is that it **releases heat** as part of the functioning of a nuclear power station.

47. B
The natural polymer described is **protein** (poly amino acid/polypeptide).

Cellulose and starch are natural polymers of glucose that do not contain nitrogen. Nylon is a synthetic polymer that contains nitrogen.

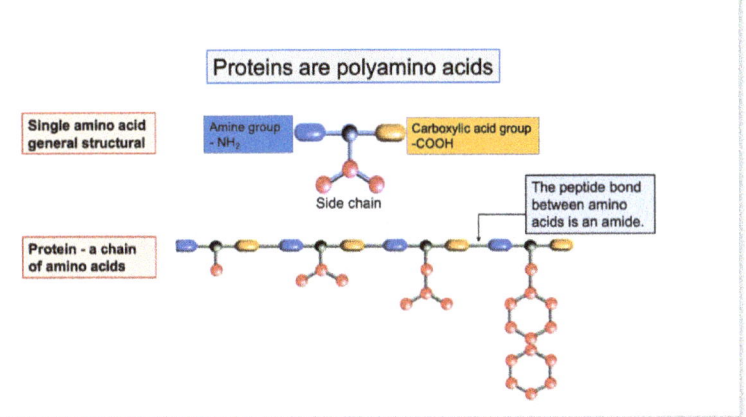

48. C
45 g of ethanoic acid must be dissolved in 500 ml of water to make a **1.5 M** solution.

A 1.5 M solution by definition contains 1.5 moles in one litre of solution.
1.5 moles of ethanoic acid is 60 g x 1.5 = 90 g.
90 g of ethanoic acid dissolved in one litre of water would make a 1.5 M solution.
Therefore, 45 g of ethanoic acid in 500 ml of water would also create a 1.5 M solution.

49. C
Only **compounds** (e.g. methane) can be decomposed - elements cannot be decomposed.

Methane is a compound but iodine, iron and germanium are elements.

50. B
A **beta particle** is an **electron**.

Therefore, an electron does not have the mass of one or two atomic mass units. Nor does it have the mass of an alpha particle.

Test Three

1. What shape is the methane molecule?

○ A. Cube
○ B. Sphere
○ C. Tetrahedron
○ D. Rectangle

2. What is the mass of a neutron?

○ A. 0 atomic mass units
○ B. 1 atomic mass unit
○ C. 2 atomic mass units
○ D. 3 atomic mass units

3. Which of the following elements most easily accepts an extra electron?

○ A. He
○ B. Ca
○ C. Cl
○ D. V

4. Butane contains _____ carbon atom(s).

○ A. 1
○ B. 2
○ C. 3
○ D. 4

5. The solubility of calcium chloride in 100 ml of water at 25 ºC is 35 g. This means that:

○ A. The maximum mass of calcium chloride that can dissolve in 100 ml of water is 35 g at 25 ºC.
○ B. The minimum mass of calcium chloride that can dissolve in 100 ml of water is 35 g at 25 ºC.
○ C. The maximum mass of calcium chloride that can dissolve in 1000 ml of water is 35 g at 25 ºC.
○ D. The maximum mass of calcium chloride that can dissolve in 100 ml of water is 35 g at 20 ºC.

6. Each column in the periodic table is a:

○ A. Group
○ B. Period
○ C. Diagonal
○ D. Horizontal

7. An acid is a compound that:

○ A. Produces hydroxide ions (OH⁻) in water.
○ B. Produces hydrogen atoms (H) in water.
○ C. Produces hydrogen ions (H⁺) in water.
○ D. Produces chloride ions (Cl⁻) in water.

8. A chemical reaction produces heat. So the reaction must be:

○ A. Endothermic
○ B. Exothermic
○ C. Endothalmic
○ D. Exothalmic

9.

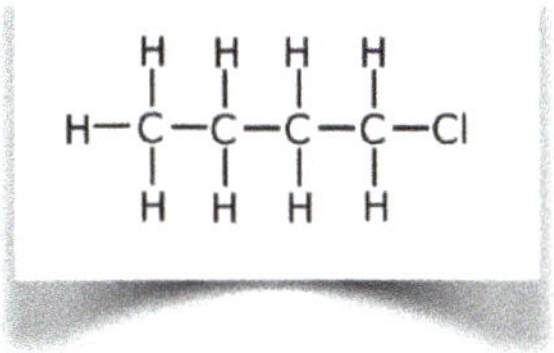

$$H-\underset{\underset{H}{|}}{\overset{\overset{H}{|}}{C}}-\underset{\underset{H}{|}}{\overset{\overset{H}{|}}{C}}-\underset{\underset{H}{|}}{\overset{\overset{H}{|}}{C}}-\underset{\underset{H}{|}}{\overset{\overset{H}{|}}{C}}-Cl$$

What kind of compound is shown above?

○ A. Halocarbon
○ B. Ester
○ C. Alcohol
○ D. Carboxylic acid

10. Early scientists decided that the beam in a cathode tube consisted of negatively charged particles because the ray:

○ A. Was deflected by target nuclei.
○ B. Was able to change colours depending on the gas in the cathode tube.
○ C. Was attracted to positively charged plates.
○ D. Was moved by a magnetic field.

11. What is the name of the compound MgF_2?

○ A. Difluoromethane
○ B. Difluoromagnesium
○ C. Carbon fluoride
○ D. Magnesium fluoride

12. Which of the following sequences lists the elements in the order of decreasing atomic radius?

- A. Li > Be > B > N > F
- B. Be > Li > N > B > F
- C. F > B > N > Li > Be
- D. B > N > F > Li > Be

13. Which of the elements is not an alkali metal?

- A. Ca
- B. Cs
- C. Na
- D. Rb

14. Which of the following processes is not a chemical reaction?

- A. Baking fresh bread.
- B. Mixing a salad dressing.
- C. Lighting a match.
- D. Rusting of iron.

15. Which of these molecules is a dipole?

- A. H-H
- B. D-D
- C. H-F
- D. Br-Br

16. A mole of any ideal gas occupies approximately 22.4 L at standard temperature and pressure (0 °C and 1 atm). The molecular mass of H_2 is 2 g/mol. What is the volume occupied by 8 g of $H_{2(g)}$ at 0 °C and 1 atm?

- A. 22.4 L
- B. 67.2 L
- C. 112 L
- D. 89.6 L

17. The orange juice that you drank during breakfast was pH 4. The concentration of hydrogen ions in the orange juice was:

- A. 1×10^{-2} M
- B. 1×10^{-3} M
- C. 1×10^{-4} M
- D. 1×10^{-5} M

18. Which one of the chemical reactions below is correctly balanced?

- A. $C_5H_{12} + 8O_2 \Rightarrow 3CO_2 + 3H_2O$
- B. $C_5H_{12} + O_2 \Rightarrow 16CO_2 + H_2O$
- C. $C_5H_{12} + 8O_2 \Rightarrow 5CO_2 + 6H_2O$
- D. $C_5H_{12} + 4O_2 \Rightarrow 5CO_2 + 6H_2O$

19. If you put a sealed air balloon in hot water the balloon expands in size. This is a practical example of:

- A. Charles' law
- B. Boyle's law
- C. Newton's law
- D. Ohm's law

20. For which of the compounds below is the mass percentage of carbon 10%?
(Atomic masses: C = 12, H = 1, Cl = 35.5)

- A. CCl_4
- B. $CHCl_3$
- C. CH_2Cl_2
- D. CH_3Cl

21. How many moles of phosphorus pentachloride are required to produce 146 grams of hydrogen chloride when the yield of the reaction is 80%?
(Atomic masses: P = 31, N = 14, H = 1, Cl = 35.5)

$PCl_{5(g)} + 5NH_{3(g)} \Rightarrow P(NH_2)_{5(s)} + 5HCl_{(g)}$

- A. 80 moles
- B. 5 moles
- C. 3 moles
- D. 1 mole

22. The empirical formula of trichlorobenzene is C_2HCl and its molecular mass is 181.5 g. What is trichlorobenzene's molecular formula? (Atomic masses: C = 12, H = 1, Cl = 35.5)

- A. $C_6H_6Cl_6$
- B. $C_6H_3Cl_3$
- C. $C_2H_1Cl_1$
- D. $C_4H_2Cl_2$

23. What kind of compound is $H_2C=CH_2$?

- A. An alkyne
- B. An alkene
- C. An alkane
- D. A plastic

24. Which change is most likely to decrease a chemical reaction rate?

- A. Lowering the temperature.
- B. Adding an enzyme.
- C. Increasing the concentration of the reactants.
- D. Adding a catalyst.

25. What is the general shape of C_6H_6?

- A. Tetrahedron
- B. Sphere
- C. Circle
- D. Rectangle

26. What is the ionization equilibrium constant (K_i) expression for the acid below?

$$HCl_{(aq)} \rightleftharpoons H^+_{(aq)} + Cl^-_{(aq)}$$

- A. $K_i = [H^+][Cl^-] / [HCl]$
- B. $K_i = [H^+][Cl^-] / [HCl][H^+]$
- C. $K_i = [HCl] / [H^+][Cl^-]$
- D. $K_i = [H^+][Cl^-] / [H^+][Cl^-]$

27. What is the product **X** of this nuclear reaction?

$$^{239}_{94}Pu + {}^{4}_{2}He \Rightarrow {}^{242}_{95}Am + X$$

- A. Proton
- B. Neutron
- C. Alpha particle
- D. Electron

28. What is the maximum number of electrons that can be held in an *f* subshell?

- A. 18
- B. 14
- C. 7
- D. 6

29. A neutral unexcited atom of an element has the electronic configuration $1s^2 2s^2 2p^6 3s^2 3p^6$. What is the atomic number of the atom?

- A. 16
- B. 22
- C. 20
- D. 18

30. Which of the compounds below is a weak acid?

- A. $CH_3COOH_{(aq)}$
- B. $HCl_{(aq)}$
- C. $HNO_{3(aq)}$
- D. $H_2SO_{4(aq)}$

31. Zinc is above copper in the redox activity series for metals in water. Which of the reactions below is most likely to occur?

- A. $Zn + CuSO_4 \Rightarrow ZnSO_4 + Cu$
- B. $Cu + ZnSO_4 \Rightarrow CuSO_4 + Zn$
- C. $ZnCl_2 + Cu \Rightarrow Zn + CuCl_2$
- D. $Cu + Zn(NO_3)_2 \Rightarrow Cu(NO_3)_2 + Zn$

32. An unknown compound has a high melting point, conducts electricity when melted, dissolves well in water and conducts electricity well in aqueous solution. This compound is likely to be a(n):

- A. Ionic compound
- B. Covalent compound
- C. Noble gas
- D. Benzene

33. Fizzy drinks/carbonated drinks or sodas are created by dissolving carbon dioxide in the liquid. Under what conditions will the carbon dioxide gas be most soluble?

- A. High temperature and high pressure.
- B. Low temperature and high pressure.

- C. Low temperature and low pressure.
- D. High temperature and low pressure.

34. Dry ice contains mainly:

- A. Nitrogen
- B. Oxygen
- C. Carbon dioxide
- D. Water

35. Entropy is:

- A. An increase in order and a decrease in randomness.
- B. A decrease in order and an increase in randomness.
- C. A decrease in spontaneously occurring processes.
- D. Decreasing in the universe with time.

36. Which of the following substances is likely to undergo sublimation spontaneously?

- A. $H_{2(g)}$ at room temperature and pressure.
- B. $CO_{2(s)}$ at room temperature and pressure.
- C. $H_2O_{(l)}$ at room temperature and pressure.
- D. $Fe_{(s)}$ at room temperature and pressure.

37. What is the chemical formula of sodium hydrogen carbonate?

- A. $NaHCO_3$
- B. Na_2CO_3
- C. $NaHSO_4$
- D. Na_2SO_4

38. At room temperature and pressure a negative Gibbs free energy ($\triangle G$) suggests that the chemical reaction is:

- A. Not spontaneous
- B. Spontaneous
- C. Fast
- D. Endothermic

39. In the periodic table the element carbon is in:

- A. Group IA

- B. Group IIA
- C. Group IIIA
- D. Group IVA

40. $CH_4 + 2O_2 => CO_2 + 2H_2O$
The above reaction is an example of:

- A. Combustion
- B. Decomposition
- C. Synthesis
- D. Single displacement

41. Ahmed buys a carton of "pure orange juice" from a local shop. After reading the ingredients he realizes that the fruit juice is 60% by volume fresh orange juice and 40% by volume of added water. The carton has a total volume of 330 ml. How much *fresh orange juice* was originally in the carton?

- A. 60 ml
- B. 150 ml
- C. 198 ml
- D. 330 ml

42. Which of the following is not a form of radiation commonly released from nuclei?

- A. Beta particles
- B. Alpha particles
- C. Gamma rays
- D. Sound waves

43. The half-life of Carbon-10 is 20 seconds. If there are initially 200 g of Carbon-10, how much Carbon-10 will remain in 40 seconds?

- A. 200 g
- B. 100 g
- C. 50 g
- D. 25 g

44. The anion Cl^- is called:

- A. Chloride
- B. Chlorate
- C. Chlorite
- D. Chloric

45. A student has conducted a titration by adding 20 ml of an unknown concentration of $NaOH_{(aq)}$ to 20 ml of 1 M $HNO_{3(aq)}$. What is the molar concentration of $NaOH_{(aq)}$?

- A. 1 M
- B. 2 M
- C. 3 M
- D. 4 M

46. Milk is a:

- A. Solution
- B. Suspension
- C. Colloid
- D. Solid

47. What is the maximum possible number of electrons in the *s* subshell of an atom?

- A. 2
- B. 4
- C. 6
- D. 8

48. Which of the following cannot be used to detect an acid?

- A. Universal indicator
- B. Blue litmus paper
- C. Red litmus paper
- D. Phenolphthalein

49. Separating crude oil components by fractional distillation is successful because they have different:

- A. Boiling points
- B. Melting points
- C. Freezing points
- D. Viscosities

50. Which of these elements is not a gas at room temperature and pressure?

- A. Chlorine
- B. Fluorine
- C. Carbon
- D. Hydrogen

TEST THREE

ANSWER SECTION

Test Three - Answer Key									
1)	C	11)	D	21)	D	31)	A	41)	C
2)	B	12)	A	22)	B	32)	A	42)	D
3)	C	13)	A	23)	B	33)	B	43)	C
4)	D	14)	B	24)	A	34)	C	44)	A
5)	A	15)	C	25)	C	35)	B	45)	A
6)	A	16)	D	26)	A	36)	B	46)	C
7)	C	17)	C	27)	A	37)	A	47)	A
8)	B	18)	C	28)	B	38)	B	48)	C
9)	A	19)	A	29)	D	39)	D	49)	A
10)	C	20)	B	30)	A	40)	A	50)	C

1. C

The carbon atom in **methane** is equally bonded to four equally sized hydrogen atoms; the most stable configuration is a **tetrahedon**.

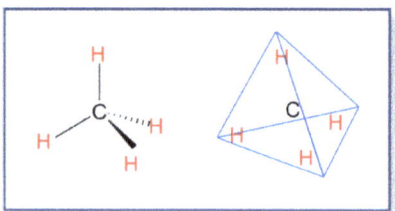

Tetrahedral structure of methane (CH₄)

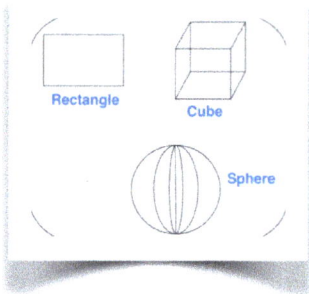

2. B

The mass of the neutron is **one atomic mass unit**.

The mass of a neutron is essentially the same as the mass of a proton - one atomic mass unit. One atomic unit is equal to one twelfth (1/12) of the mass of the most common isotope of carbon, carbon-12.

Atomic Mass Unit: $1 \text{ u} = 1.66 \times 10^{-27}$ kg

Common Atomic Masses:
○ Proton = 1.007276 u
○ Neutron = 1.008665 u
● Electron = 0.00055 u
Hydrogen 1.007825 u

3. C

Chlorine only requires a single further electron to complete its orbital and outer subshell and so become stable: $1s^2 2s^2 2p^6 3s^2 3p^5$. Chlorine is also the most electronegative atom in the list and will attract electrons.

In contrast, all of the other atoms require more than one more electron to completely full the relevant subshells in their electronic configurations:

He $1s^2 \mathbf{2s^0}$
Ca $1s^2 2s^2 2p^6 3s^2 3p^6 4s^2 \mathbf{3d^0}$
V $1s^2 2s^2 2p^6 3s^2 3p^6 4s^2 \mathbf{3d^3}$

Furthermore, the metals **calcium** and **vanadium** most readily form cations and so more easily lose electrons (oxidation) than gain electrons (reduction).

4. D

Butane contains **four** carbon atoms.

Name of straight chain alkane		Number of carbon atoms
Methane	CH₄	One
Ethane	C₂H₆	Two
Propane	C₃H₈	Three
Butane	C₄H₁₀	Four
Pentane	C₅H₁₂	Five
Hexane	C₆H₁₄	Six
Heptane	C₇H₁₆	Seven
Octane	C₈H₁₈	Eight
Nonane	C₉H₂₀	Nine
Decane	C₁₀H₂₂	Ten

A wise student should learn the names of the first ten alkanes.

5. A
The question stem implies that **maximum mass** of calcium chloride that can dissolve in 100 ml of water is 35 g at 25 °C.

> Solubility is defined as the maximum amount of **solute** that can be dissolved in a known amount of **solvent** at *equilibrium*, at a fixed temperature and pressure.

6. A
Each column in the periodic table is a **group** of elements that have similar chemical properties because of their similar electronic configurations and valencies.

> **Learn** the names of each of the **major groups** in the periodic table and their basic **chemical properties**.

7. C
An **acid** is a compound that produces **hydrogen ions (H^+)** in water (the hydrogen ions immediately bind to nearby water molecules to form *hydronium ions*).

The question stem refers to both an Arrhenius and a Brønsted-Lowry acid:

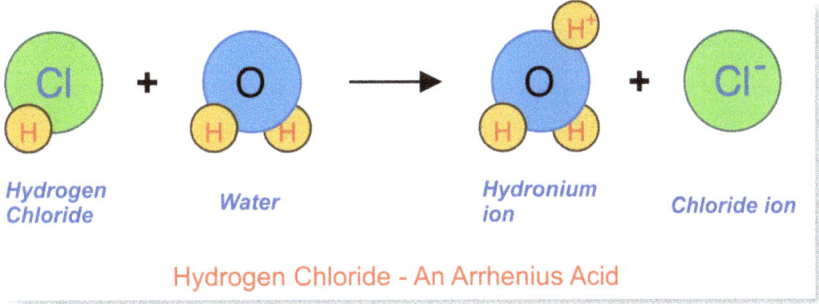

Hydrogen Chloride - An Arrhenius Acid

An **Arrhenius acid** by definition produces **hydrogen ions** in water - so here the *HCl* is an Arrhenius acid. A **Brønsted-Lowry acid** is by definition any compound that is a **proton donor** - as protons are being donated to water in the above diagram, this means that the **hydrogen chloride** is also behaving as a **Brønsted-Lowry** acid.

In contrast, **Arrhenius bases** produce hydroxide ions (OH^-) in water. The production of chloride ions in water is not part of the definition of either an acid nor a base. Nor is the production of hydrogen **atoms**.

8. B
The definition of an **exo**thermic reaction is a chemical reaction that **produces** heat.

An **endo**thermic reaction takes **in** heat. Endothalmic and exothalmic are terms that do not exist in chemistry.

9. A
The depicted compound is a **halocarbon**.

Halocarbons or haloalkanes are organic compounds containing the functional group **- C - X** where **X** may be any halogen (**F, Cl, Br, I, At**).

10. C
The question stem is essentially describing Thomson's beam experiments that supported his model of the atom - the **negatively charged particles** were **electrons** being attracted towards **positively charged plates**.

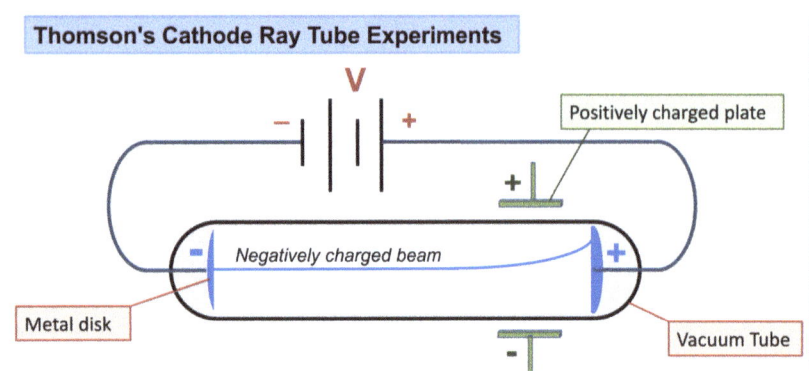

Thomson's experiments were the first to identify the electron.

11. D
MgF_2 is **magnesium fluoride**. This is an *ionic* compound.

Difluoromethane is CH_2F_2. This is an *organic* compound.
Carbon fluoride is carbon tetrafluoride, CF_4. This is an *organic* compound.

12. A
Option **A** correctly gives the sequence of elements in the **lithium period** of the periodic table.

The **atomic radius decreases** because the **increase in nuclear charge** (increase in number of protons) across the period produces a greater attractive force on the electrons in the atomic subshells.

13. A
Calcium (Ca) is not an alkali metal.

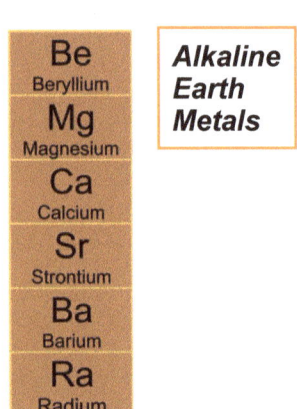
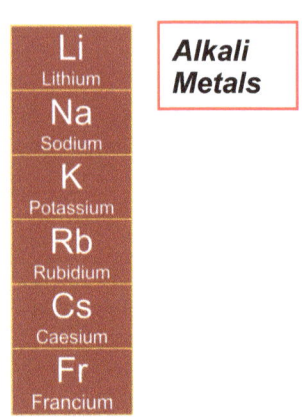

14. B
Mixing a salad dressing is a physical effect **not a chemical reaction**.

A **salad dressing** is usually created by **mixing** an oil (e.g. olive oil) with a mild aqueous acid (vinegar or lemon juice). This is a physical process.
Baking bread requires raising the temperature so structural proteins (e.g. gluten) and enzymes are denatured. This is a chemical reaction.
Rusting of elemental iron involves the oxidation of iron in air to create **iron oxides**. This is a chemical reaction.
Lighting a match involves **combustion** of flammable chemicals in the head of the match. This is a series of chemical reactions.

15. C
Hydrogen fluoride is an asymmetric compound and so is a dipole.

All of the other molecules offered as answers are symmetrical and so are nonpolar (not dipoles).

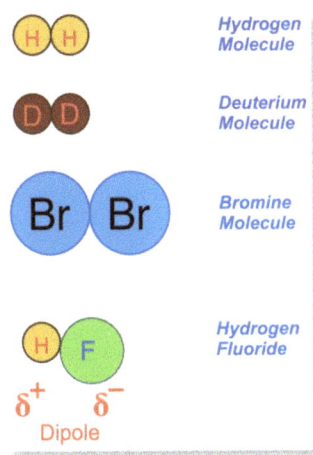

- **Symmetrical** molecules have the same and equal attraction for the orbital electrons. So, the electron cloud is evenly distributed - no part is more positive or negative than any other part.

- **Asymmetrical** molecules like HCl are dipoles because there is a difference in electronegativity between the atoms. Here the very electronegative chlorine attracts electrons more, so this part of the molecule is slightly more negative (δ-) than the hydrogen atom end of the molecule (δ+).

16. D
There are **four moles** of hydrogen gas and this is equivalent to **89.6 L** at standard temperature and pressure.

As a mole of any ideal gas occupies approximately 22.4 L at standard temperature and pressure (0 °C and 1 atm), then 4 moles (8 g/2 g) must have a volume of **4 x 22.4 = 89.6 L**.
This and similar questions assume that hydrogen is an ideal gas.

17. C
The concentration of **hydrogen ions** in the orange juice was 1×10^{-4} M.

pH is a logarithmic scale that measures hydrogen ion concentrations:
$pH = -\log_{10}[H^+]$

pH 0	pH 1	pH 2	pH 3	pH 4	pH 5	pH 6	pH 7	pH 8	pH 9	pH 10	pH 11	pH 12	pH 13	pH 14
$[H^+]=$ 1 M	$[H^+]=$ 10^{-1} M	$[H^+]=$ 10^{-2} M	$[H^+]=$ 10^{-3} M	$[H^+]=$ 10^{-4} M	$[H^+]=$ 10^{-5} M	$[H^+]=$ 10^{-6} M	$[H^+]=$ 10^{-7} M	$[H^+]=$ 10^{-8} M	$[H^+]=$ 10^{-9} M	$[H^+]=$ 10^{-10} M	$[H^+]=$ 10^{-11} M	$[H^+]=$ 10^{-12} M	$[H^+]=$ 10^{-13} M	$[H^+]=$ 10^{-14} M

(Similar colour changes occur with universal indicator).

18. C
Option **C** equation is correctly balanced:

$$C_5H_{12} + 8O_2 \Rightarrow 5CO_2 + 6H_2O$$

Left side of the chemical equation: **5C**   Right side of the chemical equation: **5C**
                                    12H   **12H**
                                    16O   **16O**

The number of atoms of each type is the same on both sides of the chemical equation *so the chemical reaction is balanced*.

19. A
The question stem demonstrates a practical example of **Charles' law**.

Boyle's law relates the pressure of an ideal gas to its volume. Ohm's law is commonly expressed as V=IR. Newton's laws relate to the physics of motion.

20. B
The mass percentage of carbon in **CHCl$_3$ is 10%**.

CCl_4 => Mass percentage of carbon:
12 / 12 + (35.5 x 4) = **7.8%**
CH_2Cl_2 => Mass percentage of carbon:
12 / 12 + 2 + (35.5 x 2) = **14%**
CH_3Cl => Mass percentage of carbon:
12 / (12 + 3 + 35.5) = **24%**

21. D
1 mole of phosphorus pentachloride is required.

The *molar mass* of hydrogen chloride is 36.5 g. 146/36.5 = **4 moles of hydrogen chloride**.
As four moles of this product represents 80% of the expected yield, 100% yield would be **five** moles of hydrogen chloride.

The stoichiometry of the reaction is shown below:
PCl$_{5(g)}$ + 5NH$_{3(g)}$ => P(NH$_2$)$_{5(s)}$ + 5HCl$_{(g)}$
  1   **5**

For this complete and balanced reaction **1 mole of phosphorus pentachloride** is required to produce these 5 moles of hydrogen chloride.

22. B
Trichlorobenzene's molecular formula is **C$_6$H$_3$Cl$_3$**.

To calculate the molecular formula:
(Atomic masses: C = 12, H = 1, Cl = 35.5)
Empirical mass of C_2HCl = 24 + 1 + 35.5 = 60.5
Molecular mass = 181.5 g
=> **181.5/60.5 = 3**
So, the molecular mass is three times the empirical mass.
=> **3 x C$_2$HCl = C$_6$H$_3$Cl$_3$**

23. B
$H_2C=CH_2$ is an **alkene**:

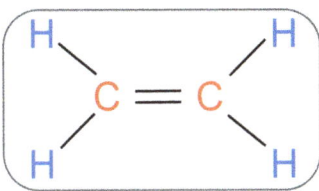

Ethene has the *alkene* functional group of C=C.

24. A
Lowering the temperature would generally decrease a chemical reaction rate.

Lowering the temperature **decreases the thermal/kinetic energy** of the **reactants**, so that fewer of the chemicals have enough energy to overcome the **activation energy** barrier for the reaction.

In contrast, using an enzyme or **catalyst would lower the activation energy barrier** for the reaction and so more reactants have enough energy to overcome the activation energy barrier - so increasing the chemical reaction rate. Increasing the concentration of reactants increases the chemical reaction rate by **increasing** the number of atomic/molecular **collisions** that will yield successful reactions.

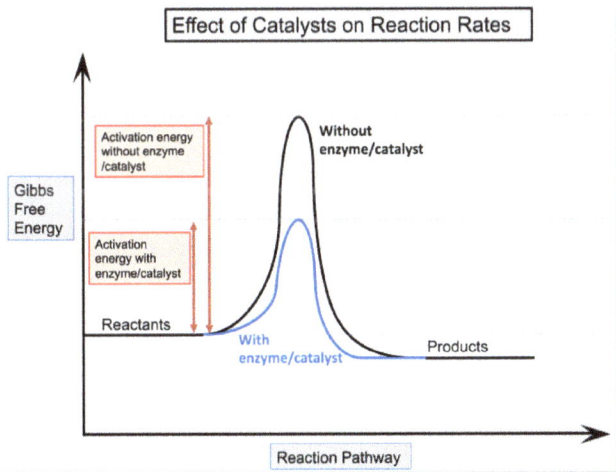

25. C
The general shape of C_6H_6 **is circular**.

C_6H_6 is benzene:

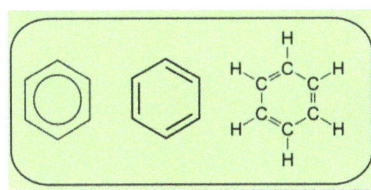

Kekule was the first to suggest the circular structure of benzene.

26. A
The correct expression is $K_i = [H^+][Cl^-] / [HCl]$ for the reaction below:

$$HCl_{(aq)} \rightleftharpoons H^+_{(aq)} + Cl^-_{(aq)}$$

27. A
The product **X** of the nuclear reaction below is a **proton**.

$$^{239}_{94}Pu + ^{4}_{2}He \Rightarrow ^{242}_{95}Am + X$$

Because 239 + 4 = 242 + 1
and 94 + 2 = 95 + 1

So => $^{1}_{1}X = ^{1}_{1}p$

28. B
The maximum number of electrons that can be held in an **f** subshell is **14**.

All students should memorize the names and number of electrons that each atomic subshell can hold.

29. D
The atomic number of an element with the electronic configuration $1s^2 2s^2 2p^6 3s^2 3p^6$ is **18**.

In a neutral atom there is no overall charge so the number of protons must be equal to the number of electrons - the electronic configuration indicates 18 electrons. This means 18 protons must be present in the nucleus.

30. A
Ethanoic acid/acetic acid, $CH_3COOH_{(aq)}$, is a **weak acid**.

Hydrochloric acid, nitric acid and sulphuric acid are strong acids because they almost **completely dissociate** in water to yield **hydronium ions** and the respective bases. Ethanoic acid is a weak acid because it does not completely dissociate into protons in water. Instead it forms an **equilibrium**:

$$CH_3COOH_{(aq)} \rightleftharpoons CH_3COO^-_{(aq)} + H^+_{(aq)}$$

31. A
The most likely reaction is $Zn + CuSO_4 \Rightarrow ZnSO_4 + Cu$.

As zinc is higher than copper in the **redox activity series** in aqueous solution, zinc will be oxidized and copper ions will be reduced. Only reaction **(A)** describes oxidized zinc and reduced copper ions.

The Redox Activity Series		
$Li_{(s)} \Rightarrow Li^{+}_{(aq)} + e^{-}$	Oxidation reaction	Increasing ease of oxidation ↑
$K_{(s)} \Rightarrow K^{+}_{(aq)} + e^{-}$	Oxidation reaction	
$Ba_{(s)} \Rightarrow Ba^{2+}_{(aq)} + 2e^{-}$	Oxidation reaction	
$Ca_{(s)} \Rightarrow Ca^{2+}_{(aq)} + 2e^{-}$	Oxidation reaction	
$Mg_{(s)} \Rightarrow Mg^{2+}_{(aq)} + 2e^{-}$	Oxidation reaction	
$Zn_{(s)} \Rightarrow Zn^{2+}_{(aq)} + 2e^{-}$	Oxidation reaction	
$Fe_{(s)} \Rightarrow Fe^{2+}_{(aq)} + 2e^{-}$	Oxidation reaction	
$Cu_{(s)} \Rightarrow Cu^{2+}_{(aq)} + 2e^{-}$	Oxidation reaction	
$Ag_{(s)} \Rightarrow Ag^{2+}_{(aq)} + 2e^{-}$	Oxidation reaction	
$Pt_{(s)} \Rightarrow Pt^{2+}_{(aq)} + 2e^{-}$	Oxidation reaction	

32. A
The question stem describes the physical and chemical properties of an **ionic compound.**

Ionic compounds have high melting points, conduct electricity when melted, dissolve well in water and conduct electricity well in aqueous solution. **Covalent compounds** generally do not conduct electricity well and often do not dissolve well in water.

33. B
Gas in liquid solutions show the highest gas solubility when the **pressure is high and the temperature is low**.

The best way to remember this is to remember that your glass of Pepsi, Coke, lemonade or carbonated water is most fizzy (and tastiest!) when it is coldest. The higher pressure physically forces more gas into solution by affecting the equilibrium following Le Chatelier's principle. *With increasing pressure:*

$$CO_{2(g)} \rightleftharpoons CO_{2(aq)}$$

34. C
Dry ice is frozen carbon dioxide and so is composed of **carbon dioxide**.

Frozen water is ice. The commonest (laboratory) cold form of nitrogen is liquid nitrogen and similarly the commonest cold form of oxygen is liquid oxygen.

35. B
Entropy is a decrease in order with an **increase in randomness**.

Chemical reactions occur either with an increase in entropy or with entropy staying the same. Gibbs free energy, a measure of whether a chemical reaction will occur spontaneously, depends on entropy according to the following expression:

ΔG = ΔH + TΔS
Gibbs free energy change (**ΔG**) = **Enthalpy** change (**ΔH**) + (Absolute temperature x **Entropy** change, **TΔS**)

36. B
$CO_{2(s)}$ at room temperature and pressure undergoes spontaneous **sublimation**.

Sublimation is the phase change **directly from solid to gas**. Substances that commonly sublime at room temperature and pressure include dry ice, iodine, arsenic and naphthalene.

37. A
The chemical formula of sodium hydrogen carbonate is **NaHCO₃**.

Sodium hydrogen carbonate is the same as **sodium bicarbonate**:

38. B
At room temperature and pressure a **negative Gibbs free energy** (△G) indicates that the chemical reaction is **spontaneous**.

A chemical reaction with a **negative Gibbs free energy** (△G) is termed **exergonic**. **Endothermic** is used to refer to a **positive enthalpy** (△H) - which is a reaction that absorbs heat.

39. D
Carbon is in **Group IVA** of the periodic table.

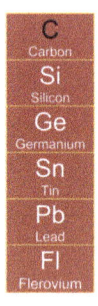

Group IVA elements have carbon as the first element.

40. A
The reaction CH₄ + 2O₂ => CO₂ + 2H₂O is an example of **combustion**.

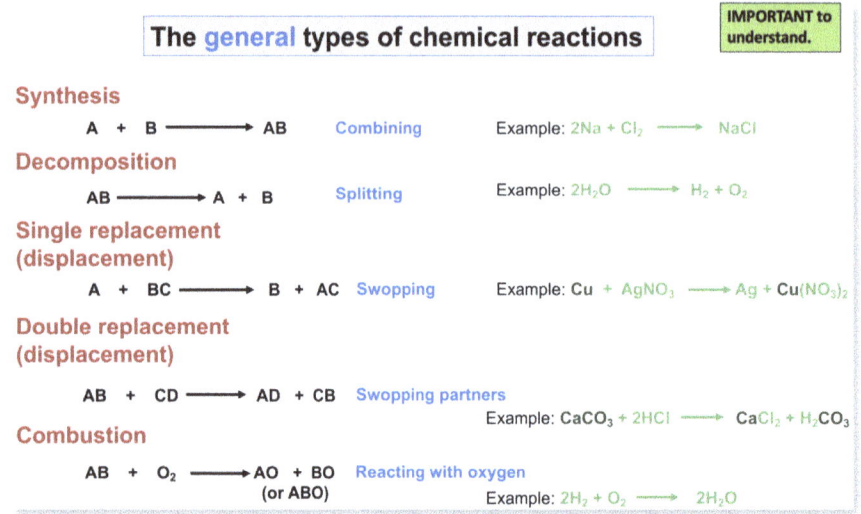

41. C
Originally, **198 ml of fresh orange juice** was in the 330 ml carton.

To calculate the *volume* of fresh orange juice:
60% x 330 ml => **198 ml**

42. D
Sound waves are **not a form of nuclear radiation**.

Sound waves are **longitudinal mechanical waves** whereas nuclear radiation takes the form of either electromagnetic transverse waves (gamma rays) or subatomic particles (e.g. alpha particles or electrons).

Common forms of nuclear radiation:

Characteristics of Nuclear Radiation				
Radiation Type	Symbol	Charge	Mass (amu)	Common Sources
Alpha particle	α $^4_2$He	+2	4	Radium-226
Beta particle	β $^0_{-1}$e	-1	0.000544	Carbon-14
Gamma ray	γ	0	0	Cobalt-60

43. C
After 40 seconds only **50 grams** of the original 200 grams of Carbon-10 will remain.

The definition of half-life is the time taken for half the number of radioactive nuclide originally present to disintegrate. So, after 20 seconds the quantity of Carbon-10 atoms will drop from 200 grams to 100 grams. After a further 20 seconds the quantity of Carbon-10 atoms will drop from 100 grams to 50 grams.

Radioactive decay can also be calculated using the expression below:

$$N = N_o e^{-\lambda t}$$

N_o is the initial quantity of radioactive nuclides, **N** is the final quantity of radioactive nuclides, λ is the decay constant, **t** is elapsed time (time allowed for decay) and **e** is the Euler constant 2.71828.

44. A
The anion Cl⁻ is called **chloride**.

In contrast the other structures are:
Chlorate => **ClO$_3^-$**
Chlorite => **ClO$_2^-$**
Chloric (acid) => **HClO$_3$**

45. A
The molar concentration of **NaOH$_{(aq)}$ is 1 M**.

NaOH$_{(aq)}$ + HNO$_{3(aq)}$ => NaNO$_{3(aq)}$ + H$_2$O$_{(l)}$
   1   1   1   1   *(Stoichiometry)*

So, for this complete titration reaction 20 ml of *1 molar sodium hydroxide* are required to neutralize 20 ml of 1 molar nitric acid, in order to balance this reaction.

46. C
Milk is a **colloid**.

Milk is cloudy and uniform throughout - it cannot be separated into its components by filtration:

	Solutions	Suspensions	Colloids
Appearance	Clear	Cloudy	Cloudy
Consistency	Uniform and constant throughout.	Not uniform and separates/settles on standing.	Uniform and constant throughout.
Particle size	Less than 1 nm in diameter.	More than 100 nm in diameter.	1 - 100 nm in diameter.
Filtration	Cannot be separated by filtration.	Can be separated by filtration.	Cannot be separated by filtration.
Examples	Saline/salt water	Salad dressing	Milk

47. A
The maximum possible number of electrons in the **s** subshell of an atom is **two**.

s subshell => maximum of two electrons
p subshell => maximum of six electrons
d subshell => maximum of ten electrons
f subshell => maximum of fourteen electrons

48. C
Red litmus paper cannot be used to detect an acid - it is used to **detect bases and then turns blue**.

Universal indicator is a mixture of indicators that change colour according to the pH and so can be used to detect acids. **Phenolphthalein** is a useful pH indicator that turns from pink to colourless in the presence of acids. Finally, **blue litmus paper** is good for detecting acids and turns red in their presence.

49. A
Separating crude oil components by fractional distillation is successful because they have different **boiling points**.

Fractional distillation is effective because the liquids **vaporize separately at their boiling points** and are then condensed separately. Melting points, freezing points and viscosities do not allow for such effective and convenient separation of liquids.

50. C
Carbon is not a gas at room temperature and pressure, it is a solid in all of its allotropic forms.

Fluorine, chlorine and hydrogen are gases at room temperature and pressure.

EmSAT Chemistry Achieve   Dr Sinclair Steele

Test Four

1. The shape of AlCl$_3$ is

- A. Tetrahedral
- B. Trigonal planar
- C. Linear
- D. Circular

2. Which of the following is not a chemical property?

- A. Taste
- B. Smell
- C. Density
- D. Reactivity with acid

3. Which of the following is true about bases?

- A. A base has a pH greater than 7.
- B. A base has a pH of 7.
- C. A base has a pH less than 7.
- D. Bases are present in car batteries.

4. Complete the sequence:
Methane, Ethane, Propane, Butane, Pentane, Hexane, _____, Octane.

- A. Hexane
- B. Nonane
- C. Heptane
- D. Decane

5. Which of the following would not increase the speed/rate of dissolving sugar in a cup of tea?

- A. Cooling the tea.
- B. Heating the water for the tea.
- C. Decreasing the size of the sugar lumps.
- D. Stirring the tea.

6. What happens to the atomic radius of the elements in a group of the periodic table, as the group is descended?

- A. It decreases.
- B. It increases.

○ C. It remains the same.
○ D. It increases then decreases.

7. How many electrons are in the nucleus of a hydrogen atom?

○ A. None
○ B. One
○ C. Two
○ D. Three

8.

What kind of compound is shown above?

○ A. Halocarbon
○ B. Ester
○ C. Alcohol
○ D. Carboxylic acid

9. Each horizontal row in the periodic table is a:

○ A. Group
○ B. Period
○ C. Diagonal
○ D. Horizontal

10. A solution that contains *more* of the dissolved solute than should be dissolved under normal circumstances at that temperature and pressure is:

○ A. An unsaturated solution.
○ B. A saturated solution.
○ C. A supersaturated solution.
○ D. Pure water.

11. What type of nuclear reaction is shown?

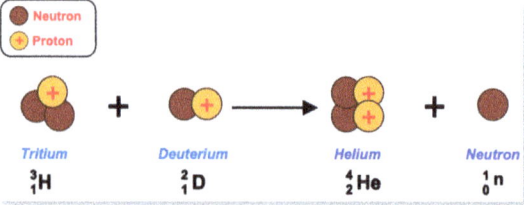

- A. Fission
- B. Fusion
- C. Gamma emission
- D. Neutron absorption

12. An element that can exist in two or more physical forms has multiple:

- A. Allotropes
- B. Isotopes
- C. Radioisotopes
- D. Nuclei

13. Which of the following will be most attracted to a negatively charged plate?

- A. Alpha particles
- B. Electrons
- C. Hydrogen atoms
- D. Neutrons

14. Ionic bonds

- A. are effective because of shared electrons.
- B. are effective because of magnetic properties.
- C. are effective because of opposite charges.
- D. are effective because of neutron numbers.

15. Compared to the charge on a proton the neutron's charge is:

- A. Greater and the same sign.
- B. Equal and the same sign.
- C. Lesser and closer to neutral.
- D. Lesser and more positive.

16. What is the correct description of the chemical below?

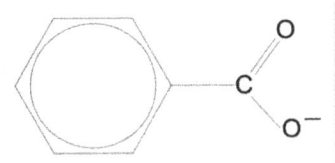

- A. Cation
- B. Anion

○ C. Molecule
○ D. Phenol

17. Nitrogen has the atomic number seven. Which of the following is its electronic configuration?

○ A. $1s^2 2s^2 2p^6 3s^2$
○ B. $1s^2 2s^2 2p^6$
○ C. $1s^2 2s^2 2p^2$
○ D. $1s^2 2s^2 2p^3$

18. Water boils when

○ A. its vapour pressure is equal to the melting point.
○ B. its vapour pressure is equal to the freezing point.
○ C. its vapour pressure is less than the surrounding atmospheric pressure.
○ D. its vapour pressure is equal to the surrounding atmospheric pressure.

19. Which of the following elements is most chemically similar to oxygen?

○ A. Hydrogen
○ B. Sulphur
○ C. Titanium
○ D. Chlorine

20. Which of the following is the most electronegative atom?

○ A. Li
○ B. B
○ C. C
○ D. O

21. Hydrogen bonds are important in the physical properties of which substance?

○ A. Bromine
○ B. Hydrogen
○ C. Water
○ D. Benzene

22. Which of the following is not an accepted assumption regarding the properties of an ideal gas?

○ A. Gas particles move randomly, quickly and continuously.
○ B. There are no attractive forces between the gas particles.

- C. The collisions between the gas particles are perfectly elastic.
- D. Gas particles are very large and occupy a large space.

23. A base is a compound that

- A. produces hydroxide ions (OH-) in water.
- B. produces hydrogen atoms (H) in water.
- C. produces hydrogen ions (H+) in water.
- D. produces chloride ions (Cl-) in water.

24. What is the correct classification of the elements iron, nickel, silver and gold?

- A. Metalloids
- B. Transition metals
- C. Alkali metals
- D. Alkaline earth metals

25. Which of the following is not an electrolyte in water?

- A. HBr
- B. NaCl
- C. NaOH
- D. C_2H_5OH

26. If the chemical formula of a solute is known what other information is needed to calculate the molarity of the solution?

- A. Mass of the solvent.
- B. Mass of the solute dissolved.
- C. Volume of the solvent used and mass of the solvent used.
- D. Mass of the solute dissolved and final volume of the solution.

27. What is the new pressure of a fixed mass of hydrogen gas in a 500 ml vessel at 297 K and 1.1 atmosphere when heated to 64 °C and compressed to 250 ml?

- A. (1.1) x (0.5) x (24) / (64) x (0.25)
- B. (1.1) x (0.5) x (337) / (297) x (0.25)
- C. (297) x (0.25) / (1.1) x (0.5) x (337)
- D. (64) x (0.25) / (1.1) x (0.5) x (24)

28. Which of the following is the strongest acid?

- A. Propanoic acid, $K_a = 1 \times 10^{-5}$
- B. Hydrocyanic acid, $K_a = 5 \times 10^{-9}$
- C. Benzoic acid, $K_a = 6.5 \times 10^{-5}$
- D. Carbonic acid, $K_a = 4.3 \times 10^{-7}$

29. Acetone is often used to remove nail polish. If a bottle containing 50 millilitres of nail polish remover has 40% of acetone by volume, how much acetone is in the bottle?

- A. 20 ml
- B. 25 ml
- C. 30 ml
- D. 35 ml

30. Which bond is formed by the equal sharing of electrons?

- A. Dipole - dipole
- B. Ionic
- C. Covalent
- D. Van der Waals

31. Which of the following samples of molecules contain the most number of moles?

- A. 30 g of CO_2
- B. 30 g of N_2
- C. 30 g of CCl_4
- D. 30 g of H_2

32. Which statement describes how a catalyst changes the rate of a reaction?

- A. The catalyst increases $\triangle G$ of the reaction.
- B. The catalyst increases $\triangle H$ of the reaction.
- C. The catalyst increases the activation energy, E_A, of the reaction.
- D. The catalyst decreases the activation energy, E_A, of the reaction.

33. What is the molarity of a solution made by dissolving 45 g of KNO_3 in water to make a 600 ml solution? (KNO_3 has a molecular mass of 101 g/mol).

- A. 0.54 M
- B. 0.64 M
- C. 0.74 M
- D. 0.84 M

34. What is the pH of an aqueous solution if the [H⁺] = 0.00001 M?

○ A. 1
○ B. 5
○ C. 8
○ D. 12

35. Which of the following is the reason why water has an unexpectedly high boiling point compared to hydrogen sulphide?

○ A. Covalent bonds
○ B. London forces
○ C. Hydrogen bonds
○ D. Ionic bonds

36. Which of the following is not used to measure pressure?

○ A. Pascals
○ B. Rascals
○ C. mmHg
○ D. Atmospheres

37. Choose the correctly balanced equation for the reaction:

$$C_6H_6 + O_2 \Rightarrow CO_2 + H_2O$$

○ A. $2C_6H_6 + 15O_2 \Rightarrow 6CO_2 + 3H_2O$
○ B. $C_6H_6 + 3O_2 \Rightarrow 6CO_2 + 3H_2O$
○ C. $2C_6H_6 + 15O_2 \Rightarrow 12CO_2 + 6H_2O$
○ D. $C_6H_6 + 6O_2 \Rightarrow 6CO_2 + 3H_2O$

38. Identify the item that becomes reduced in the following redox reaction:

$$Sn^{2+}_{(aq)} + HgBr_{2(aq)} \Rightarrow Sn^{4+}_{(aq)} + Br^{-}_{(aq)} + Hg_2Br_{2(s)}$$

○ A. $HgBr_{2(aq)}$
○ B. $Hg_2Br_{2(s)}$
○ C. $Sn^{2+}_{(aq)}$
○ D. $Sn^{4+}_{(aq)}$

39. Fructose (fruit sugar) has a molar mass of 180 g/mol and has an empirical formula of CH_2O. What is the molecular formula of fructose?
(Molar masses: Carbon 12 g/mol, Hydrogen 1 g/mol, Oxygen 16 g/mol).

- A. C4H8O4
- B. C9H18O9
- C. C6H12O6
- D. C3H6O3

40. If the specific heat capacity of copper is 0.4 joules/g°C, which of the following statements is not true?

- A. 0.4 joules of heat energy is required to raise the temperature of 1 g of copper by 1 °C.
- B. 0.4 joules of heat energy will raise 2 g of copper by a temperature of 0.5 °C.
- C. 0.8 joules of heat energy will raise 2 g of copper by a temperature of 0.5 °C.
- D. 0.8 joules of heat energy will raise 2 g of copper by a temperature of 1 °C.

41. Which of the following is the most reactive element?

- A. Calcium
- B. Neon
- C. Krypton
- D. Xenon

42. A student mixes two elements together and a chemical reaction occurs that absorbs heat. The reaction is:

- A. Endothermic
- B. Exothermic
- C. Endocaloric
- D. Exocaloric

43. At normal room temperature and pressure magnesium is a:

- A. Gas
- B. Liquid
- C. Solid
- D. Plasma

44. The aluminium in aluminium chloride is in which form?

- A. Al^+
- B. Al^{2+}
- C. Al^{3+}
- D. Al^{4+}

45. CO_3^{2-} is called:

○ A. Bicarbonate
○ B. Nitrate
○ C. Sulphate
○ D. Carbonate

46. When CH_3COOH reacts with C_2H_5OH in the presence of acid the products are:

○ A. A salt and water
○ B. A salt and hydrogen gas
○ C. An acid and a base
○ D. An ester and water

47. Which of the following statements about the reaction below is not true?

$$^{235}_{92}U + ^{0}_{1}n \longrightarrow ^{236}_{92}U \longrightarrow ^{141}_{36}Ba + ^{92}_{36}Kr + 3\,^{1}_{0}n$$

○ A. This reaction occurs in nuclear bombs.
○ B. This is an endothermic reaction.
○ C. This reaction can be used in nuclear power stations.
○ D. This reaction has a negative enthalpy.

48. What kind of compound is HC≡CH?

○ A. An alkyne
○ B. An alkene
○ C. An alkane
○ D. A plastic

49. A synthetic polymer that contains only carbon, hydrogen and oxygen and is present in large amounts in clothing is most likely to be:

○ A. Polyester
○ B. Protein
○ C. Starch
○ D. Cellulose

50. A glass bottle of lemonade is dropped but remains intact. You suspect that there may now be some glass fragments in the lemonade. Which process will most easily separate the glass fragments from the lemonade?

○ A. Sublimation

○ B. Filtration
○ C. Chromatography
○ D. Freezing

TEST FOUR

ANSWER SECTION

Test Four - Answer Key									
1)	B	11)	B	21)	C	31)	D	41)	A
2)	C	12)	A	22)	D	32)	D	42)	A
3)	A	13)	A	23)	A	33)	C	43)	C
4)	C	14)	C	24)	B	34)	B	44)	C
5)	A	15)	C	25)	D	35)	C	45)	D
6)	B	16)	B	26)	D	36)	B	46)	D
7)	A	17)	D	27)	B	37)	C	47)	B
8)	D	18)	D	28)	C	38)	A	48)	A
9)	B	19)	B	29)	A	39)	C	49)	A
10)	C	20)	D	30)	C	40)	C	50)	B

1. **B**
The shape of AlCl$_3$ is **trigonal planar**:

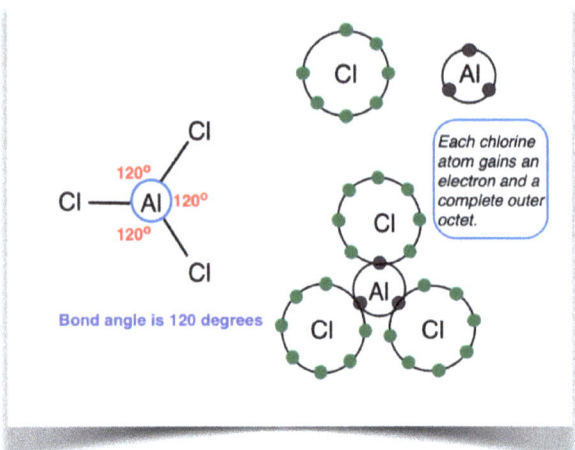

A trigonal planar structure allows the chlorine atoms to have maximum separation from each other - and so this AlCl$_3$ structure is more stable.

2. **C**
Density is a **physical property** not a chemical property.

Obviously, *reacting* with an acid is a **chemical** process. *Taste* and *smell* involve **chemical** reactions between molecules/polyatomic ions and **receptors** in cell membranes.

3. **A**
Arrhenius bases produce hydroxide ions (OH⁻) in water and so there are more hydroxide ions present than hydronium ions present. This makes the **pH greater than 7**.

Pure water at normal room temperature (25 °C) is pH 7 and is neither an acid nor a base - it is neutral. Neutrality is a more general term that is defined as the condition where [H⁺] = [OH⁻]. The pH of neutrality can change with temperature.

Bases are not usually present in **car batteries** - commonly, **sulphuric acid** is present in car batteries.

4. **C**
Methane, Ethane, Propane, Butane, Pentane, Hexane, **HEPTANE**, Octane.

This is the beginning of the alkane homologous series:

Name of straight chain alkane		Number of carbon atoms
Methane	CH$_4$	One
Ethane	C$_2$H$_6$	Two
Propane	C$_3$H$_8$	Three
Butane	C$_4$H$_{10}$	Four
Pentane	C$_5$H$_{12}$	Five
Hexane	C$_6$H$_{14}$	Six
Heptane	C$_7$H$_{16}$	Seven
Octane	C$_8$H$_{18}$	Eight
Nonane	C$_9$H$_{20}$	Nine
Decane	C$_{10}$H$_{22}$	Ten

5. A
Cooling the tea will **not increase** the rate of sugar dissolving in the tea.

Heating the tea increases the number of particles with enough energy to overcome the activation energy for the reaction, and so increases the rate of dissolving. **Stirring the tea** increases the rate of mixing and so increases the speed of dissolving. **Decreasing the size of the sugar lumps** increases the surface area to volume ratio - and so increases the space for the reactants to meet. This too will increase the rate of dissolving.

6. B
The effect of the increasing subshell number is greater than the effect of the increase in atomic number, so the **atomic radius increases** as the group is descended.

This can be explained because (a) the outermost electrons are further away from the nucleus and (b) the additional inner subshells also provide *shielding* from the electrical attraction between the nucleus and these outer electrons.

7. A
The neutral hydrogen atom contains only **one electron:**

The hydrogen atom has atomic number one and so has a single proton and a single electron in the neutral atom.

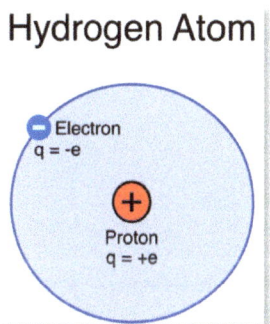

8. D
The image shows the structural formula of a **carboxylic acid** (propanoic acid).

Carboxylic acids are organic compounds with the **functional group -COOH**:

Name of straight chain carboxylic acid		Number of carbon atoms
Methanoic acid	HCOOH	One
Ethanoic acid	CH_3COOH	Two
Propanoic acid	C_2H_5COOH	Three
Butanoic acid	C_3H_7COOH	Four
Pentanoic acid	C_4H_9COOH	Five
Hexanoic acid	$C_5H_{11}COOH$	Six
Heptanoic acid	$C_6H_{13}COOH$	Seven
Octanoic acid	$C_7H_{15}COOH$	Eight
Nonanoic acid	$C_8H_{17}COOH$	Nine
Decanoic acid	$C_9H_{19}COOH$	Ten

9. B
Each horizontal row in the periodic table is called a **period**.

The vertical columns are called groups. There is no name for diagonal lines in the periodic table.

10. C
A solution that contains *more* of the solute than should be dissolved under normal circumstances of temperature and pressure is termed **supersaturated**.

Supersaturated solutions are created by dissolving large amounts of solute into a hotter solvent and then cooling it. This created solution, with an excessive amount of solute, is actually not stable ("*metastable*"). So, addition of seed crystals can result in precipitation of the extra solute from this supersaturated solution and so convert the supersaturated solution into a saturated solution.

11. B
Tritium and deuterium combine to form a single nucleus and therefore this is a nuclear **fusion** reaction.

When the fused nuclei are small then generally the **fusion reactions are exothermic**. Accordingly, research into fusion reactions is important because they could be a future source of abundant and relatively clean energy.

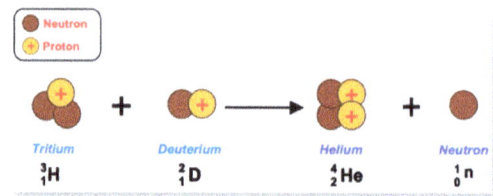

12. A
Allotropes are elements that can exist in two or more physical forms. (For example, diamond and graphite are allotropes of carbon).

A radioisotope is a radioactive isotope - the nucleus emits radiation. Allotropes are generally not radioactive. Isotopes generally have the same form (solid, liquid or gas) but different numbers of neutrons in the nuclei. Some isotopes are radioactive.

13. A
A negatively charged plate will attract positively charged particles such as **alpha particles**.

Electrons are negatively charged and so will be repulsed by a negatively charged plate. Neutrons are uncharged and so will be unaffected by a negatively charged plate. Hydrogen atoms are also uncharged.

14. C
Ionic bonds are effective because of **opposite charges**.

The opposite charges on the ions lead to attraction between the ions. **Cations** are positively charged and **anions** are negatively charged.

> Students are advised to learn and remember that
> **cations** are positively charged (usually metallic ions) and
> **anions** are negatively charged (usually non-metal ions).

15. C
Compared to the charge on a proton the neutron's charge is **lesser and closer to neutral**.

This is because the electron has one unit of negative charge whereas the neutron has no charge.

16. B
This is a polyatomic ion (benzoate) that is negatively charged. So, it is an **anion**.

A *molecule* is a polyatomic compound that is **uncharged**, however benzoate is negatively **charged**. Notice that the phenol molecule is also uncharged.

17. D
Nitrogen has the atomic number seven and so the electronic configuration of the neutral atom is **$1s^2\ 2s^2\ 2p^3$**.

The atomic number of the neutral atom is also the same as the number of its electrons.

18. D
Water boils when its vapour pressure is **equal to the surrounding atmospheric pressure**.

As water is heated the **vapour pressure of the liquid increases** until it is the same as the atmospheric pressure - **then it boils:**

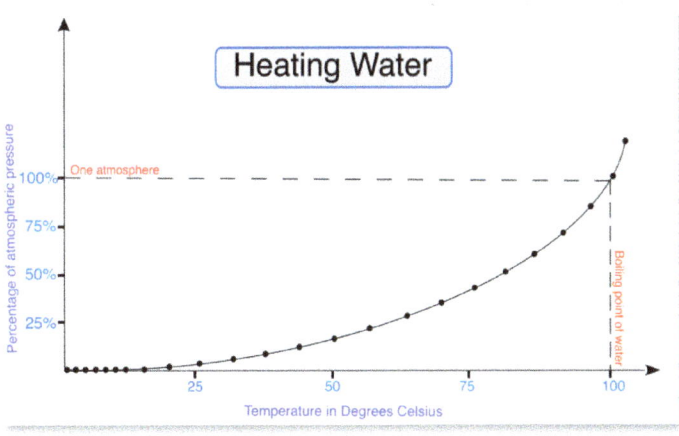

19. B
Sulphur is most chemically similar to oxygen because they are in the same group of the periodic table.

The electronic configurations of their outermost subshells are similar and lead to similar reactions and reactivity. Oxygen => $1s^2 2s^2 2p^4$, Sulphur => $1s^2 2s^2 2p^6 3s^2 3p^4$

Group VIA elements

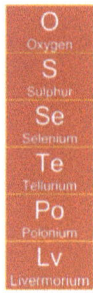

20. **D**
Oxygen is the most electronegative atom.

Electronegativity can be defined as the tendency/probability of an atom in a covalent bond to attract the bonding electrons. It is a measure of the attractive force between the *positively* charged *nucleus* of an element and the *negatively* charged *shared electrons*. **Electronegativity increases from left to right across a period in the periodic table - making oxygen the most electronegative answer option**. Electronegativity also increases while moving up a group in the periodic table.
In part because of the inertness of the noble gases and their lack of electron sharing, the most electronegative atom in the periodic table is **actually fluorine**.

21. **C**
Hydrogen bonds are important in determining the **physical properties of water** - they explain the higher than expected boiling point of water, its high specific heat capacity, high heat of vaporization, increased surface tension and water's ability to dissolve a range of solutes.

Bromine, hydrogen and *benzene* cannot form hydrogen bonds.

A hydrogen bond is a weak intermolecular force that occurs under the following conditions:

i) A **hydrogen atom** is covalently **bonded to a very electronegative atom** (most commonly oxygen, nitrogen or fluorine), making a relative dipole:

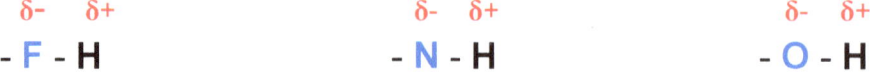

ii) The relatively positive (δ+) **hydrogen end of the dipole is attracted to relatively negative (δ-) atoms** in other molecules/ions. These electronegative atoms in other molecules/ions are also either oxygen, nitrogen or fluorine. For example:

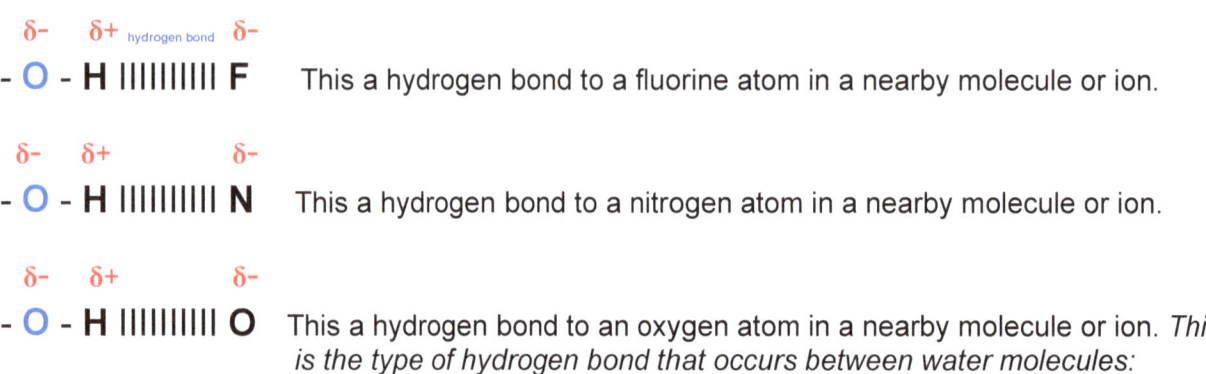

- O - H |||||||||| F   This a hydrogen bond to a fluorine atom in a nearby molecule or ion.

- O - H |||||||||| N   This a hydrogen bond to a nitrogen atom in a nearby molecule or ion.

- O - H |||||||||| O   This a hydrogen bond to an oxygen atom in a nearby molecule or ion. *This is the type of hydrogen bond that occurs between water molecules:*

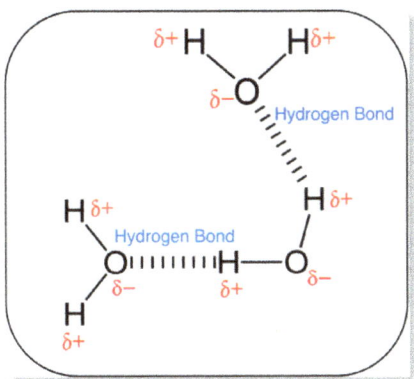

Hydrogen bonds are approximately only a tenth the strength of a covalent bond.

22. D
Ideal gas particles are *not* supposed to **be very large and occupy a large space**.

Ideal gas particles should move randomly, quickly and continuously. There should be no attractive forces between the gas particles in an ideal gas. The collisions between the gas particles in an ideal gas should be completely elastic. **Finally, the particles in an ideal gas should be very small and occupy little space.**

> For the EmSAT exam it is important to know these **assumptions** or essential properties of an **ideal gas**.

23. A
The Arrhenius definition of a base is a compound that **produces hydroxide ions (OH⁻) in water**. For example:

$KOH_{(s)} + H_2O_{(l)} => K^+_{(aq)} + OH^-_{(aq)}$

24. B
Iron, nickel, silver and gold are **transition metals**.

A **transition metal** is an element whose electronic configuration **has a partially filled *d* subshell**, or that can make positively charged ions with an **incomplete *d* subshell**:

Fe (iron) $1s^2 2s^2 2p^6 3s^2 3p^6 4s^2 3d^6$

Ni (nickel) $1s^2 2s^2 2p^6 3s^2 3p^6 3d^8 4s^2$

Ag (silver) $1s^2 2s^2 2p^6 3s^2 3p^6 3d^{10} 4s^2 4p^6 4d^{10} 5s^1$
   Ag^{2+} $1s^2 2s^2 2p^6 3s^2 3p^6 3d^{10} 4s^2 4p^6 4d^9$

Au (gold) $1s^2 2s^2 2p^6 3s^2 3p^6 3d^{10} 4s^2 4p^6 4d^{10} 4f^{14} 5s^2 5p^6 5d^{10} 6s^1$
   Au^{3+} $1s^2 2s^2 2p^6 3s^2 3p^6 3d^{10} 4s^2 4p^6 4d^{10} 4f^{14} 5s^2 5p^6 5d^8$

> The **d** subshells can contain a maximum of **ten** electrons.

A **metalloid** has the chemical and physical properties intermediate between a metal and a non-metal. **Alkali metals** are *Group IA metals* and **alkaline earth metals** are *Group IIA metals*. In contrast, **transition metals** are found in **groups 3 - 12** (IIIB - IIB).

25. D
Ethanol (C_2H_5OH) is an organic covalent molecule that does not dissociate in water and therefore is **not an electrolyte**. In contrast, HBr, NaCl and NaOH are ionic compounds that dissociate in water and so are electrolytes.

26. D
To calculate the molarity of a solution you need to know how much solute is present and in what volume of water (in order to calculate a *concentration*). Therefore, the **mass of the solute** dissolved and **final volume of the solution** are required.

27. B
Using $P_1V_1/T_1 = P_2V_2/T_2$ the correct answer is **(1.1) x (0.5) x (337) / (297) x (0.25)**.

$$\frac{P_1V_1}{T_1} = \frac{P_2V_2}{T_2}$$

(P = pressure, V = volume, T = absolute temperature)
*When using the **Combined gas law equation** a common mistake is to forget to convert the temperature from degrees Celsius into Kelvin.*

28. C
Benzoic acid, $K_a = 6.5 \times 10^{-5}$ is the strongest acid.

Benzoic acid$_{(aq)}$ ⇌ Benzoate$_{(aq)}$ + H$^+_{(aq)}$ K_a = [Benzoate] x [H$^+$] / [Benzoic acid]

A **strong acid** is an acid that dissociates most readily (easily) into the hydrogen ion and the conjugate/ partner base. So, a strong acid will have a large K_a. Benzoic acid has the **largest K_a**.

29. A
40% of the 50 ml bottle of nail polish remover is acetone - this is **20 ml**.

50 x 0.4 => 20 ml

30. C
Covalent bonds require **equal sharing** of electrons.

Electron sharing, a *covalent bond*, happens **inside** a molecule and so is **intra**molecular. However, dipole-dipole forces and van der Waals forces act **between** molecules and so are **inter**molecular forces. No electron sharing is occurring between the molecules.

Ionic bonds involve **transferring** of electron(s) instead of sharing electrons.

31. D
The correct answer is **30g of H_2**.

To calculate the number of moles, divide 30 by the molar mass of each molecule:

A. 30 g of CO_2 =>   30/44 = 0.68 moles
B. 30 g of N_2 =>   30/14 = 2.14 moles
C. 30 g of CCl_4 =>   30/154 = 0.19 moles

D. 30 g of H_2 => 30/2 = 15 moles

32. D
A catalyst changes the rate of a reaction by **decreasing the activation energy**.

Neither the change in Gibbs free energy, $\triangle G$, nor the change in enthalpy, $\triangle H$, affect the rate of the chemical reaction, just the energetics.

33. C
The correct answer is **0.74 M**.

Number of moles of KNO_3 = 45/101 = **0.45 moles**
Total volume = **0.6 L**
Molar concentration of KNO_3 = 0.45/0.6 = **0.74 M**

34. B
An aqueous solution of $[H^+]$ = 0.00001 M has a **pH of 5**.

pH = -log$_{10}$ [H$^+$] = -log$_{10}$[0.00001] = **5**

35. C
The correct answer is **hydrogen bonds**.

Water can form **hydrogen bonds** but hydrogen sulphide cannot. Hydrogen sulphide forms weaker dipole-dipole **inter**molecular bonds.

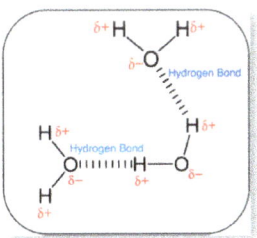

36. B
Rascals are not a measure of pressure.

Pascals, mmHg and atmospheres are all measures of pressure.

37. C
$2C_6H_6 + 15O_2 => 12CO_2 + 6H_2O$ is correctly balanced.

Left side of the chemical equation: **12**C   Right side of the chemical equation: **12**C
                                    12H   **12**H
                                    30O   **30**O

The number of atoms of each type is the same on both sides of the chemical equation *so the chemical reaction is balanced.*

38. A

HgBr₂₍aq₎ is the item that is reduced during the redox reaction.

Considering **HgBr₂₍aq₎**:

i) $HgBr_2$ is composed of Hg^{2+} and Br^-.

ii) The Hg^{2+} becomes Hg^+ during this reaction - this means that the silver +2 ion has gained an electron and so has been **reduced** to become silver +1.

iii) Br^- remains Br^-.

In contrast, during this redox reaction tin (Sn) is **oxidized** because it has lost electrons:
$Sn^{2+} => Sn^{4+} + 2e^-$

39. C
The molecular formula of fructose is $C_6H_{12}O_6$.

To calculate the molecular formula:
Empirical mass of CH_2O = 12 + 2 + 16 = 30
Molecular mass = 180 g
=> **180/30 = 6**
So, the molecular mass is six times the empirical mass.
=> **6 x CH_2O = $C_6H_{12}O_6$**

40. C
0.8 joules of heat energy will raise 2 g of copper by a temperature of 0.5 °C.

The definition of specific heat capacity is summarized in the following equations:
$Q = mc\theta$ or $q = mc\Delta T$
Q, q = Heat energy (joules)   **m** = Mass (g or kg)
θ, ΔT = Temperature change (°C)

If the specific heat capacity of copper is 0.4 joules/g°C then this means that **0.4** joules of heat energy will be required to raise 1 g of copper by a temperature of 1 °C.

=> 0.4 joules = 1 g x **0.4** x 1 °C
=> 0.8 joules = 2 g x **0.4** x 0.5 °C

41. A
Calcium is the most reactive element.

Neon, krypton and xenon are inert, unreactive noble gases. In contrast, calcium is a very reactive group IIA metal that donates two outer subshell electrons during its reactions.

Atomic number, Z	Element	Number of electrons/shell	Comment
10	Neon	2, 8	Complete and stable outer subshell.
36	Krypton	2, 8, 18, 8	Complete and stable outer subshell.
54	Xenon	2, 8, 18, 18, 8	Complete and stable outer subshell.

42. A
A reaction that absorbs heat is **endothermic**.

Exothermic reactions produce **heat**. *Exothermic* reactions have negative enthalpies (-ΔH) whereas *endothermic* reactions have positive enthalpies (+ΔH). The words *endocaloric* and *exocaloric* do not exist.

43. C
At normal room temperature and pressure magnesium is a **solid**.

Magnesium is a solid and so can be used in car seats, computers and fireworks.

44. C
Aluminium chloride, $AlCl_3$, contains aluminium in the form of **Al^{3+}**.

The **valency** of aluminium is **+3**.
The electronic configuration of aluminium is **$1s^2 2s^2 2p^6 3s^2 3p^1$**.

It is **easier for the aluminium atom to release three electrons** than to acquire five electrons to complete the p subshell.

45. D
CO_3^{2-} is called carbonate.

A. Bicarbonate => HCO_3^-
B. Nitrate => NO_3^-
C. Sulphate => SO_4^{2-}

46. D
When CH_3COOH reacts with C_2H_5OH in the presence of acid the products are an **ester and water**:

$$R_1OH + R_2COOH \xrightarrow{H^+} R_2COOR_1 + H_2O$$

    Alcohol   Carboxylic acid   Ester   Water

A. A **salt and water** are formed by the reaction between an **acid and base**.
   HX + MOH => H_2O + MX   (M = metal atom, MOH = base, MX = salt, HX = acid)
B. A **salt and hydrogen gas** are formed by the reaction between an acid and a metal.
   HX + M => $H_{2(g)}$ + MX
C. **An acid and a base** can react to form a salt and water.

47. B
This nuclear reaction is *exothermic* and **not endothermic** - this why it is used in nuclear power stations.

$$^{235}_{92}U + ^{1}_{0}n \longrightarrow ^{236}_{92}U \longrightarrow ^{141}_{56}Ba + ^{92}_{36}Kr + 3\,^{1}_{0}n$$

Exothermic reactions have negative enthalpy (-ΔH) and so option *D* is a true statement. Identical and similar reactions to the one above occur in nuclear bombs and so option *A* is a true statement.

48. A
HC≡CH is an **alkyne**. It has the **C≡C** functional group.

Homologous Series of Alkynes

Alkynes	Number of carbon atoms	Semistructural formula
Ethyne	2	HC≡CH
Propyne	3	CH_3-C≡CH
Butyne	4	CH_3-CH_2-C≡CH
Pentyne	5	CH_3-CH_2-CH_2-C≡CH
Hexyne	6	CH_3-CH_2-CH_2-CH_2-C≡CH
Heptyne	7	CH_3-CH_2-CH_2-CH_2-CH_2-C≡CH
Octyne	8	CH_3-CH_2-CH_2-CH_2-CH_2-CH_2-C≡CH
Nonyne	9	CH_3-CH_2-CH_2-CH_2-CH_2-CH_2-CH_2-C≡CH
Decyne	10	CH_3-CH_2-CH_2-CH_2-CH_2-CH_2-CH_2-CH_2-C≡CH

49. A
A synthetic polymer that contains only carbon, hydrogen and oxygen and is present in large amounts in clothing is **polyester**.

Polyester

In contrast, protein is an amino acid polymer that includes **nitrogen** atoms. Starch and cellulose are both polymers of glucose that do not contain nitrogen atoms. Starch is a carbohydrate present in many foods. Cellulose is a component of wood.

50. B
Simple physical separation by **filtration** would be most effective.

Neither glass nor water is capable of **sublimation**. **Chromatography** is more commonly used to separate coloured materials that can at least partially dissolve in water (separating between mobile and stationary phases). **Freezing** the lemonade would trap the glass fragments in ice and so not help separation.

Test Five

1. Which subatomic particle has the smallest mass?

○ A. An electron
○ B. A proton
○ C. A neutron
○ D. An alpha particle

2. Which of the following is the strongest acid?

○ A. Hydrochloric acid, pK_a = -6
○ B. Ethanoic acid, pK_a = 4
○ C. Ethyne, pK_a = 25
○ D. Ethanol, pK_a = 17

3. What is the product **X** of the nuclear reaction above?

○ A. $^{240}_{94}Pu$
○ B. $^{236}_{92}U$
○ C. $^{238}_{93}Np$
○ D. $^{244}_{96}Cm$

4. In the Bohr atom the:

○ A. electrons orbit the nucleus like planets.
○ B. electrons travel randomly outside the nucleus.
○ C. neutrons have a positive charge.
○ D. neutron has a mass of two atomic mass units.

5. In the modern periodic table, which statement is generally true?

○ A. More metals are on the left of the table and more non-metals on the right.
○ B. More non-metals are on the left of the table and more metals on the right.
○ C. Hydrogen has the atomic number five.
○ D. The elements are listed in order of decreasing atomic number moving from left to right.

6. What kind of compound is shown here?

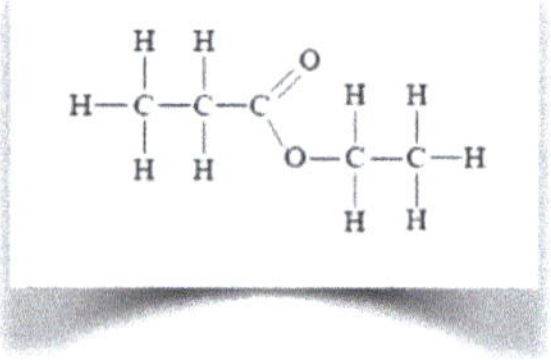

- A. Halocarbon
- B. Ester
- C. Alcohol
- D. Carboxylic acid

7. Almost all the mass of an atom exists in its:

- A. Electrons
- B. Outermost energy level
- C. Nucleus
- D. First energy level

8. What is the shape of the ammonia molecule?

- A. Tetrahedral
- B. Trigonal planar
- C. Trigonal pyramidal
- D. Linear

9. $NO_{2(g)} + SO_{2(g)} \rightleftharpoons SO_{3(g)} + NO_{(g)} +$ heat   *ΔH is negative*

Which of the changes below would shift the reaction equilibrium to the right?

- A. Increasing $SO_{3(g)}$
- B. Increasing $NO_{(g)}$
- C. Decreasing the volume of the reaction vessel
- D. Decreasing the temperature

10. What is the correct classification of the elements astatine, fluorine, iodine and bromine?

- A. Noble gases
- B. Transition metals
- C. Lanthanides
- D. Halogens

11. If the equilibrium constant, K_{eq}, is 5×10^{10} which of the following is correct?

- A. The pH is -10.
- B. The concentration of reactants equals the concentration of products.
- C. Mainly reactants are present.
- D. Mainly products are present.

12. If a chemical reaction has a ΔG that has a large negative value then which of the following is true?

- A. The reaction is not spontaneous and decreases entropy.
- B. The reaction is not spontaneous and increases entropy.
- C. The reaction is spontaneous and likely exothermic.
- D. The reaction is spontaneous and likely endothermic.

13. A liquid changes state and becomes solid. What is this process called?

- A. Sublimation
- B. Melting
- C. Evaporating
- D. Freezing

14. A calorie is a measure of:

- A. Energy
- B. Mass
- C. Volume
- D. Pressure

15. A liquid has separated into a precipitate and an overlying fluid. This fluid can be poured through a filter unchanged but the precipitate does not pass through the filter. The fluid part is best called a:

- A. Solution
- B. Suspension
- C. Colloid
- D. Supernatant

16. Chlorine has an atomic number of 17 and the neutral atom has a base electronic configuration of $1s^2 2s^2 2p^6 3s^2 3p^5$. Which electronic configuration represents an excited chlorine atom?

- A. $1s^2 2s^2 2p^6 3s^2 3p^6 3d^8 4s^2$
- B. $1s^2 2s^2 2p^6 3s^2 3p^6$
- C. $1s^2 2s^2 2p^6 3s^1 3p^6$
- D. $1s^2 2s^2 2p^6 3s^2 3p^3$

17. Mixtures are:

- A. Chemically formed.
- B. Physically formed.
- C. Biologically formed.
- D. None of the above.

18. Calculate the mass percentage of lithium in this compound: LiAlH₄.
(Atomic masses: Li = 7, Al = 27, H = 1)

○ A. 18%
○ B. 38%
○ C. 58%
○ D. 68%

19. What is the name for the experiment that led to Rutherford's Atomic Model?

○ A. Robert Hooke's microscope experiment
○ B. Gold foil experiment
○ C. Thomson's cathode ray experiment
○ D. Doppler train experiment

20. This element is a non-metal, a solid, has valency -1, is an important component of thyroid hormones and thyroid gland function, is next to bromine in the periodic table, and is not radioactive. This element is:

○ A. Chlorine
○ B. Iodine
○ C. Fluorine
○ D. Astatine

21. Which of the following is not used to make an ester?

○ A. Hydrogen ions
○ B. Propranol
○ C. Butanoic acid
○ D. Methane

22. Which of the options below correctly balances this equation?

$$Fe_{(s)} + H_2SO_{4(aq)} => Fe_2(SO_4)_{3(aq)} + H_{2(g)}$$

○ A. $2Fe_{(s)} + 3H_2SO_{4(aq)} => Fe_2(SO_4)_{3(aq)} + 3H_{2(g)}$
○ B. $Fe_{(s)} + 3H_2SO_{4(aq)} => Fe_2(SO_4)_{3(aq)} + 3H_{2(g)}$
○ C. $2Fe_{(s)} + H_2SO_{4(aq)} => Fe_2(SO_4)_{3(aq)} + H_{2(g)}$
○ D. $2Fe_{(s)} + H_2SO_{4(aq)} => Fe_2(SO_4)_{3(aq)} + 3H_{2(g)}$

23. **CH₃COO⁻** is called:

○ A. Bicarbonate

○ B. Ethanoate
○ C. Methanoate
○ D. Peroxide

24. Identify the chemical substance that would be expected to have the highest boiling point.

○ A. Polar liquid with hydrogen bonds
○ B. Polar liquid with simple dipole-dipole forces
○ C. Nonpolar liquid with London dispersion forces
○ D. Ideal gas

25. Which chemical entity does not have a trigonal planar structure?

○ A. BF_3
○ B. CO_3^{2-}
○ C. H_3O^+
○ D. SO_3

26. What is the new pressure of a fixed mass of hydrogen gas in a 750 ml vessel at 297 K and 1.0 atmosphere when heated to 64 °C and compressed to 500 ml?

○ A. (1.0) x (0.5) x (24) / (64) x (0.25)
○ B. (1.0) x (0.75) x (337) / (297) x (0.50)
○ C. (297) x (0.25) / (1.1) x (0.5) x (337)
○ D. (64) x (0.25) / (1.1) x (0.5) x (24)

27. A mole of any ideal gas occupies approximately 22.4 L at standard temperature and pressure (0 °C and 1 atm). The molecular mass of Cl_2 is 71 g/mol. What is the volume occupied by 35.5 g of $Cl_{2(g)}$ at 0 °C and 1 atm?

○ A. 22.4 L
○ B. 67.2 L
○ C. 112 L
○ D. 11.2 L

28. Fireworks are coloured because of:

○ A. The coloured organic chemicals present in the fireworks.
○ B. Their elements' group in the periodic table.
○ C. Excited electrons moving to lower energy levels.
○ D. Radioactive nuclides.

29. Halogens form anions by:

- A. Losing an electron.
- B. Gaining a neutron.
- C. Gaining one electron.
- D. Gaining two electrons.

30. Which is the chemical formula of the ammonium ion?

- A. NH_4^+
- B. NH_4^-
- C. NH_3^+
- D. NH_4^{2-}

31. Photosynthesis:

- A. Converts light energy into chemical potential energy.
- B. Converts light energy into kinetic energy.
- C. Converts potential energy into light energy.
- D. Synthesizes light from chemicals.

32. Ca_3N_2 is called:

- A. Calcium nitrate
- B. Calcium nitride
- C. Carbon nitride
- D. Calcium nitrite

33. A student has conducted a titration by adding 15 ml of an unknown concentration of $KOH_{(aq)}$ to 30 ml of 1 M $HCl_{(aq)}$. What is the molar concentration of $KOH_{(aq)}$?

- A. 1 M
- B. 2 M
- C. 3 M
- D. 4 M

34. The radioactive half-life of Iodine-131 is 8 days. How much of 1 kg of Iodine-131 will remain after 24 days?

- A. 200 g
- B. 250 g
- C. 500 g
- D. 125 g

35. Which one of the following redox processes shows reduction only?

- A. $Cu^+ \Rightarrow Cu^{2+} + e^-$
- B. $Ag_2SO_4 + Cu \Rightarrow CuSO_4 + 2Ag$
- C. $Mg \Rightarrow Mg^{2+} + 2e^-$
- D. $Na^+ + e^- \Rightarrow Na$

36. What is the total number of electrons shared in the bond between the nitrogen atoms in the azo dye molecule below?

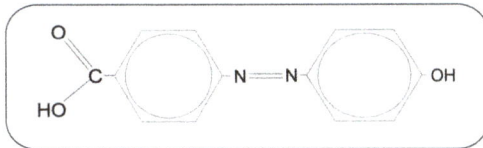

- A. 1
- B. 2
- C. 3
- D. 4

37. If the equilibrium constant, K_{eq}, for the reaction below is 1×10^6 then which of the statements is true?

$$B \rightleftharpoons A$$

- A. At equilibrium the concentration of B will be much greater than the concentration of A.
- B. At equilibrium the concentration of A will be much greater than the concentration of B.
- C. At equilibrium the concentration of B will be equal to the concentration of A.
- D. At equilibrium 75% of the chemical mixture will be B and 25% will be A.

38. What happens to the kinetic energy of an ideal gas molecule as the temperature is raised?

- A. Kinetic energy remains constant.
- B. Kinetic energy decreases.
- C. Kinetic energy increases.
- D. Kinetic energy decreases and then increases.

39. Which of the following instruments can be used to measure radioactivity?

- A. Voltmeter
- B. Geiger counter
- C. Ammeter
- D. Electron microscope

40. Which of the following statements is true?

- A. ΔS is the change in spontaneity.
- B. ΔH is the change in hydrostatic pressure.
- C. ΔG is the change in Gibbs free energy.
- D. ΔT is the change in specific heat capacity.

41. A piece of coal burns slowly in air. However, it burns brighter and faster when put in pure oxygen. Why?

- A. Oxygen is an inflammable gas.
- B. Pure oxygen can absorb the produced carbon dioxide gas.
- C. There is an increased number of collisions between carbon and oxygen.
- D. Because oxygen is more reactive at higher concentrations.

42. Potassium bromide has a mass of 119 g per mole. How many grams of potassium bromide must be added in a final volume of 500 ml to make a 1 molar aqueous solution?

- A. 59.5 g
- B. 119 g
- C. 238 g
- D. 29.8 g

43. Which of the following is an alloy?

- A. Iron
- B. Copper
- C. Tin
- D. Bronze

44. Which element has the biggest atomic number?

- A. H
- B. Li
- C. Na
- D. K

45. Which of the following is not a magnetic metal?

- A. Iron
- B. Cobalt
- C. Nickel
- D. Phosphorus

46. At normal room temperature and pressure aluminium is a:

- A. Gas
- B. Liquid
- C. Solid
- D. Plasma

47. $2H_2O \Rightarrow 2H_2 + O_2$

What type of reaction is shown above?

- A. Decomposition
- B. Single replacement
- C. Double replacement
- D. Combustion

48. Le Chatelier's principle is used for:

- A. Equilibria
- B. Nuclear reactions
- C. Catalysts
- D. Filtrations

49. Which of the following is not a carbohydrate?

- A. Glucose
- B. Fructose
- C. Starch
- D. Octane

50. The common fossil fuels are coal, petroleum and natural gas. They all contain:

- A. Hydrocarbons
- B. Plastics
- C. Carbohydrates
- D. Salt water

TEST FIVE

ANSWER SECTION

Test Five - Answer Key				
1) A	11) D	21) D	31) A	41) C
2) A	12) C	22) A	32) B	42) A
3) B	13) D	23) B	33) B	43) D
4) A	14) A	24) A	34) D	44) D
5) A	15) D	25) C	35) D	45) D
6) B	16) C	26) B	36) D	46) C
7) C	17) B	27) D	37) B	47) A
8) C	18) A	28) C	38) C	48) A
9) D	19) B	29) C	39) B	49) D
10) D	20) B	30) A	40) C	50) A

1. A
The **electron** has the smallest mass:

Particle	Component(s)	Mass - *atomic mass units*
Electron	e⁻	5.49×10^{-4} amu
Proton	p⁺	1.01 amu
Neutron	n⁰	1.01 amu
Alpha particle	n⁰p⁺ n⁰p⁺	4.0 amu

2. A
The strongest acid is **hydrochloric acid**, pK_a = -6.

A strong acid is almost completely ionized (separated into respective anions and cations) in water. So, hydrochloric acid becomes $H^+_{(aq)}$ and $Cl^-_{(aq)}$ in water. $HCl_{(g)} + H_2O_{(l)} \rightarrow H^+_{(aq)} + Cl^-_{(aq)}$

$K_a = [H^+][A^-]/[HA]$ *and* $pK_a = -\log_{10} K_a$ => **Therefore, small pK_a values mean stronger acids.**

Hydrochloric acid has the smallest pK_a and so is the strongest acid amongst the answer options.

3. B
The product **X** of the nuclear reaction below is => $^{236}_{92}U$

$$^{240}_{94}Pu \longrightarrow {^4_2}He + {^A_Z}X$$

The element X can be deduced by subtracting 4 from 240 to make 236 (mass number).

And then by subtracting 2 from 94 to make 92 (atomic number) => $^{236}_{92}U$

4. A
In the Bohr atom the electrons **orbit the nucleus like planets** orbiting the sun:

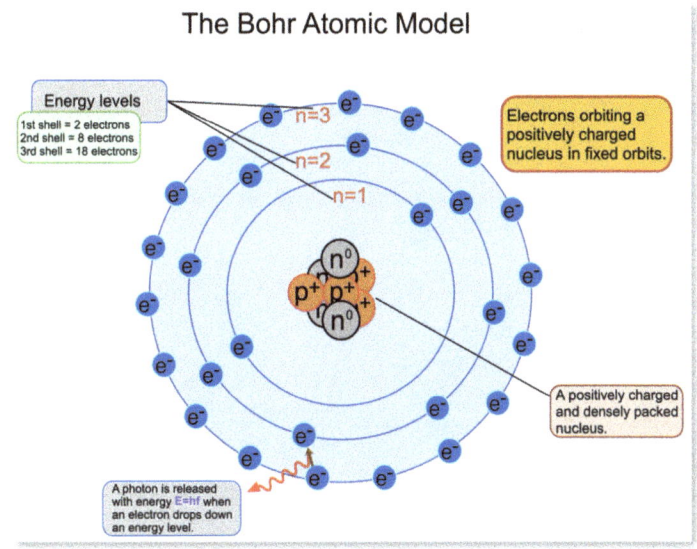
The Bohr Atomic Model

5. A
In the modern periodic table **more metals are on the left of the table** and more non-metals on the right:

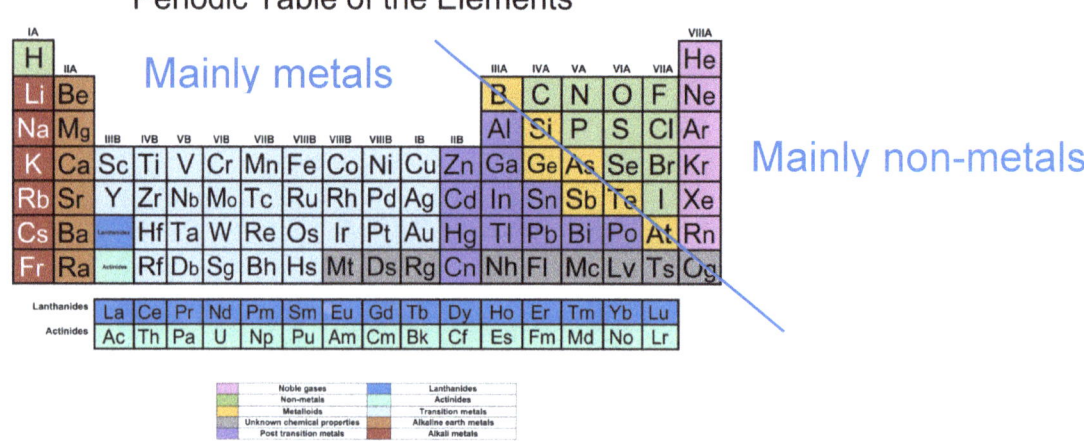

Periodic Table of the Elements

Hydrogen has **atomic number one** not five. The elements are listed in order of **in**creasing atomic number moving from left to right.

6. B
The displayed compound below is **an ester**.

Esters have the core functional group R**COO**R. The structures of *alcohol* are R-**OH**, *halocarbon* R-**X** and *carboxylic acid* R-**COOH**.

7. C
Almost all the mass of an atom exists in its **nucleus**.

This is because the protons and neutrons make up almost all the mass of the atom and they are located in the nucleus. The electrons are found outside the nucleus and have negligible mass.

8. C
The ammonia molecule has a **trigonal pyramidal** shape:

The NH_3 molecule behaves as if it has bonded to four atoms instead of the actual three. If a central atom were covalently bonded to four other identical atoms then the bond angles would all be 109.5 degrees (like methane). In the case of ammonia, the fourth "atom" is a lone electron pair - the **negatively charged** electron cloud

NH_3 - Ammonia's Trigonal pyramidal structure

produced by this electron pair *pushes against the three* N-H covalent bonds to reduce their bond angles to 107 degrees and to create the trigonal pyramidal shape.

9. D
Decreasing the temperature would shift the equilibrium of the reaction below **to the right**.

$NO_{2(g)} + SO_{2(g)} \rightleftharpoons SO_{3(g)} + NO_{(g)} + heat$ ΔH is negative

This is because Le Chatelier's principle states that an equilibrium will act to remove or decrease the effect of the added stress. Here, the added stress is cooling the reaction. The only way this equilibrium can decrease the cooling effect is to add more heat. This can be done by moving the reaction to the right, **the exothermic direction**.

Similarly, increasing the $SO_{3(g)}$ concentration would push the reaction to the left. So would increasing the $NO_{(g)}$ concentration. As the number of gas molecules (moles) on both sides of the balanced equation are the same, decreasing the volume of the reaction vessel or changing the pressure will not affect the equilibrium.

10. D
The elements astatine, fluorine, iodine and bromine are **halogens**.

The halogens are the elements of group VIIA of the periodic table:

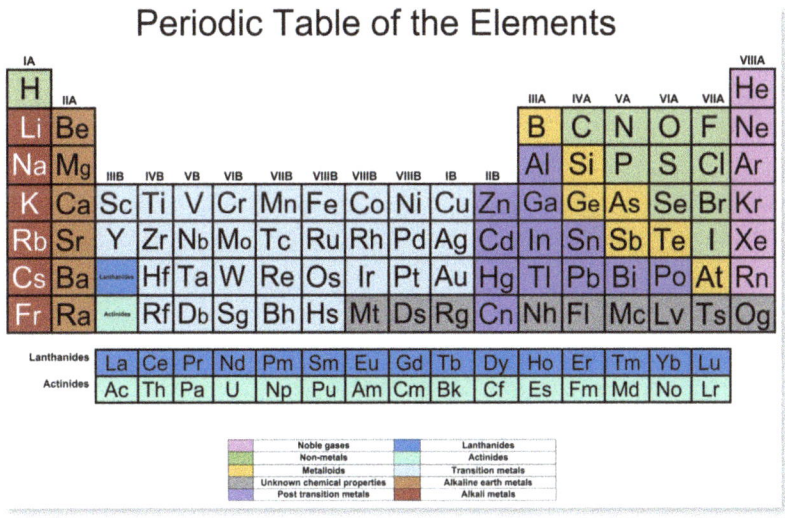

11. D
If the equilibrium constant, K_{eq}, is 5×10^{10} then **mainly products** will be present.

The value of the **equilibrium constant is so large** that the equilibrium has shifted far to the right and so nearly all the chemicals present will be products. There is no relationship between the K_{eq} and pH unless an acid is being considered - no acid is mentioned in the question stem.

12. C
A chemical reaction which has a ΔG that is large and **negative will be spontaneous and likely exothermic**.

Gibbs free energy, a measure of whether a chemical reaction will occur spontaneously, depends on entropy according to the following expression:

ΔG = ΔH + TΔS
Gibbs free energy change (**ΔG**) = **Enthalpy** change (**ΔH**) + (Absolute temperature x **Entropy** change, **TΔS**)

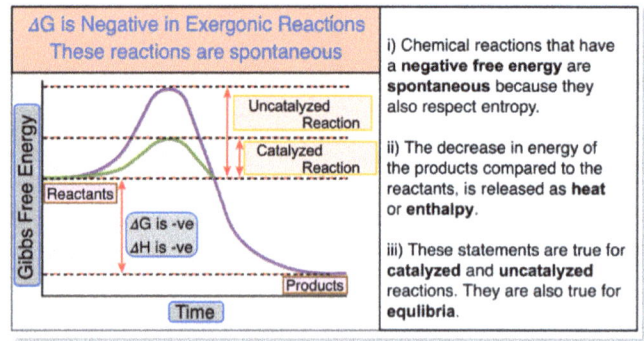

13. D
This change of state process is called **freezing**:

Phase Change	Example	Terminology (Name)
solid to liquid	Ice to water.	Melting
liquid to gas	Water to steam (water vapour).	Evaporation / Vaporization
solid to gas	1) Iodine solid to iodine vapour. 2) Dry ice (solid CO_2) to carbon dioxide gas.	Sublimation
gas to liquid	Condensation that occurs to cause rain.	Condensation
liquid to solid	Freezing of water to form ice on a cold day.	Freezing
gas to solid	Water vapour forming frost on a window.	Deposition

14. A
A calorie is a measure of **energy**.

In chemistry **energy** is usually measured in **joules, kilojoules, calories or kilocalories**. Similarly, **mass** in chemistry is usually measured in **grams or kilograms**. **Volume** in chemistry is usually measured in **litres (=cubic decimetre), cubic centimetres or millilitres**. **Pressure** is usually measured in **atmospheres, pascals or millimetres of mercury**.

15. D
The fluid component is called a **supernatant**.

The **supernatant is the clear fluid above the insoluble precipitate** - the two phases do not mix. Precipitation can occur in some chemical reactions or can occur as part of centrifugation of a mixture.

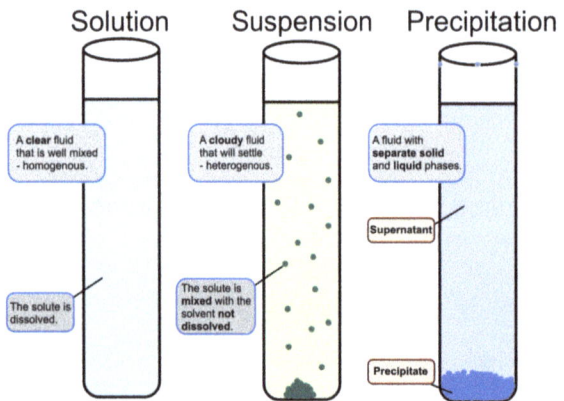

16. C
The electronic configuration of an **excited** chlorine atom is $1s^2 2s^2 2p^6 3s^1 3p^6$.

The electronic configuration of an **unexcited** chlorine atom is $1s^2 2s^2 2p^6 3s^2 3p^5$. Both the excited and unexcited chlorine atoms have 17 electrons because they both have the atomic number 17. However, the excited atom has a **3s electron** excited to the **3p subshell**.

17. B
Mixtures are **physically formed** not chemically or biologically formed.

There are no reactions occurring in physical mixtures nor does the material need to have come from biological sources.

18. A
The mass percentage of lithium in **$LiAlH_4$ is 18%.**

It can be calculated:

(Atomic masses: Li = 6.9, Al = 27, H = 1)
Atomic mass of lithium is 6.9.
Formula mass/Molar mass of **$LiAlH_4$** is 6.9 + 27 + 4 = **37.9**
Mass percentage of **Li** = 6.9/37.9 = **18%**

19. B
The experiment that led to Rutherford's Atomic Model is the **Gold foil experiment**.

Some fired **alpha particles** were **deflected/reflected** back. This was because the nuclei were positively charged and their masses were in the centre of the atom.

20. B
The element is **iodine:**

The description in the question stem is of a **halogen** (group VIIA in the periodic table).

"This element is a non-metal, a solid, has valency -1, is an important component of thyroid hormones and thyroid gland function, is next to bromine in the periodic table, and is not radioactive."

The halogen is below and next to bromine, so this is **iodine**.

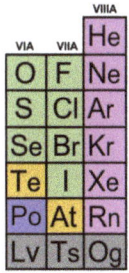

21. D
Methane is not directly used to make esters.

In contrast **hydrogen ions**, **alcohols** and **carboxylic acids** can be used to directly make esters:

$$R_1OH + R_2COOH \overset{H^+}{\rightleftharpoons} R_2COOR_1 + H_2O$$

Alcohol   Carboxylic acid   Ester   Water

22. A

This is the correctly balanced equation: $2Fe_{(s)} + 3H_2SO_{4(aq)} \Rightarrow Fe_2(SO_4)_{3(aq)} + 3H_{2(g)}$.

Left side of the chemical equation: **2Fe**   Right side of the chemical equation: **2Fe**
                                                  6H   **6H**
                                                 12O   **12O**
                                                  3S   **3S**

The number of atoms of each type is the same on both sides of the chemical equation *so the chemical reaction is balanced.*

23. B

CH_3COO^- is called **ethanoate**.

- ○ A. Bicarbonate is HCO_3^-
- ○ C. Methanoate is $HCOO^-$
- ○ D. Peroxide is O_2^-

24. A

The **polar liquid with hydrogen bonds** would be expected to have the highest boiling point.

Because such a liquid would have **the strongest bonds** amongst the answer options offered in this question:

Type of bond	Bond strength
London dispersion force	0.1 - 4 kJ/mol
Dipole - dipole bond	5 kJ - 20 kJ/mol
Hydrogen bond	4 kJ - 50 kJ/mol
Covalent bond	60 - 600 kJ/mol
Ionic bonds	560 - 1000 kJ/mol

In contrast, an ideal gas would experience only London dispersion forces and so have a low boiling point.

25. C

H_3O^+ does not have a trigonal planar structure - it has a **trigonal pyramidal** structure.

The **hydronium ion** can be considered as an oxygen atom bonded to four other atoms. The fourth "atom" is actually **a pair of electrons**. So the shape is a modified tetrahedron with similar bond angles. Here the **bond angle is 107°**. This is a **trigonal pyramidal** structure.

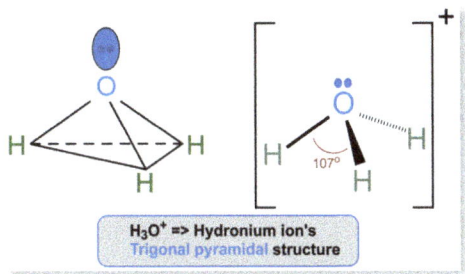

H_3O^+ => Hydronium ion's Trigonal pyramidal structure

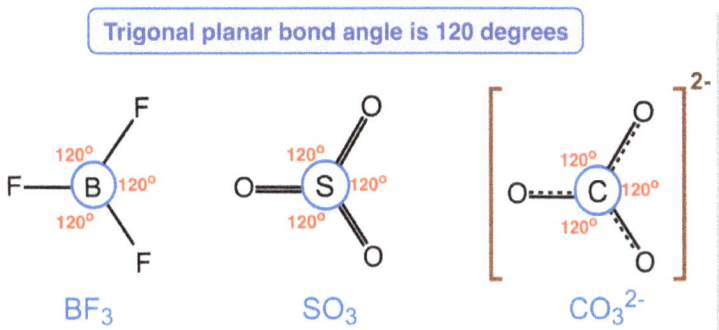

Trigonal planar bond angle is 120 degrees

BF_3 SO_3 CO_3^{2-}

26. **B**
The correct expression is (1.0) x (0.75) x (337) / (297) x (0.50).

Using $P_1V_1/T_1 = P_2V_2/T_2$ the correct answer is (1.0) x (0.75) x (337) / (297) x (0.50).

$$\frac{P_1V_1}{T_1} = \frac{P_2V_2}{T_2}$$

(P = pressure, V = volume, T = absolute temperature)

27. **D**
There is **0.5 mole** of chlorine gas and this is equivalent to **11.2 L** at standard temperature and pressure.

As a mole of any ideal gas occupies approximately 22.4 L at standard temperature and pressure (0 °C and 1 atm), then 0.5 mole (35.5 g/71 g) must have a volume of **0.5 x 22.4 = 11.2 L**.
This and similar questions assume that chlorine is an ideal gas.

28. **C**
Fireworks are coloured because of excited **electrons moving to lower energy levels** and releasing **photons of light**.

As a **firework** ignites and heats up, **electrons** gain **energy** and go up to high **energy levels**. Soon after this the **electrons** in excited atoms **drop down** to their original **energy levels**. This descent of electrons **yields photons of light energy** with each chemical's electrons undergoing *different energy level transitions* to show **characteristic colours**.

29. **C**
Halogens atoms form anions by **gaining one electron**:

Halogen	Halogen Anion
Fluorine, F_2	**Fluoride, F^-**
Chlorine, Cl_2	**Chloride, Cl^-**
Bromine, Br_2	**Bromide, Br^-**
Iodine, I_2	**Iodide, I^-**
Astatine, At_2	**Astatide, At^-**

30. **A**
The chemical formula of the ammonium ion is **NH_4^+**.

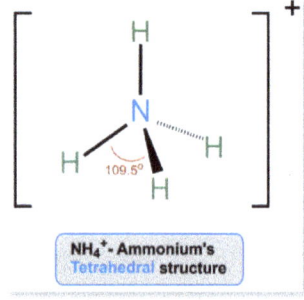

31. **A**
Photosynthesis converts **light** energy into **chemical potential energy**.

Chlorophyll is the light capturing pigment in plants that facilitates this reaction:

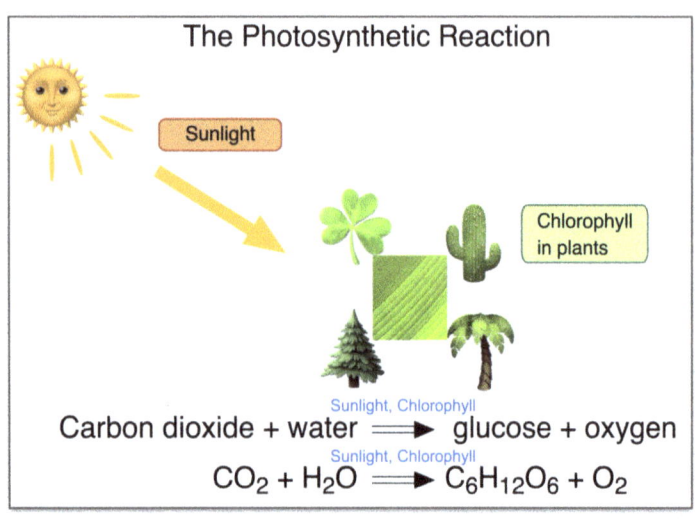

The light energy is used to make glucose. Glucose is a carbohydrate which the human body uses as a chemical energy store.

32. B
Ca$_3$N$_2$ is called **calcium nitride**.

The name of the nitrogen anion is *nitride*.

○ A. Calcium nitrate => Ca(NO$_3$)$_2$
○ C. Carbon nitride => C$_3$N$_4$
○ D. Calcium nitrite => Ca(NO$_2$)$_2$

33. B
The molar concentration of **KOH$_{(aq)}$ is 2 M**.

KOH$_{(aq)}$ + HCl$_{(aq)}$ => KCl$_{(aq)}$ + H$_2$O$_{(l)}$
  1   1   1   1   (Stoichiometry)

So, for this complete titration reaction 15 ml of two *molar potassium hydroxide* are required to neutralize 30 ml of one molar hydrochloric acid, in order to balance this reaction.

34. D
125 g of Iodine-131 will remain after 24 days:

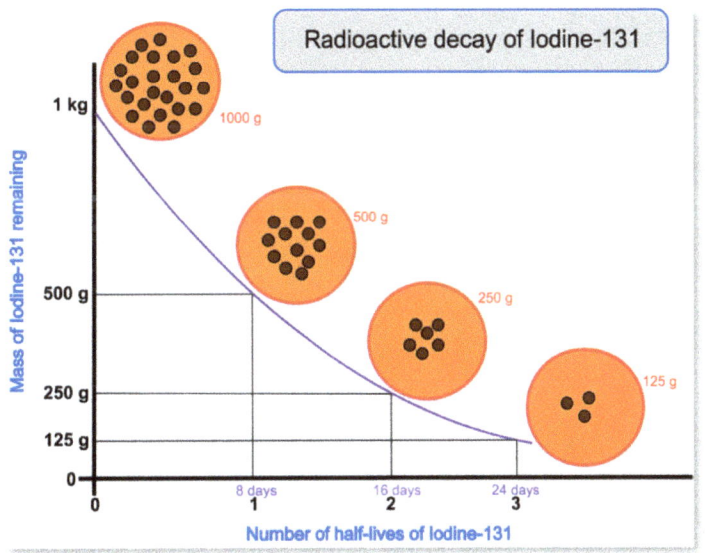

35. D
The following redox process shows reduction only: **Na$^+$ + e$^-$ => Na**.

○ A. Cu$^+$ => Cu^{2+} + e$^-$
               Oxidation of Cu$^+$

○ B. Ag$_2$SO$_4$ + Cu => CuSO$_4$ + 2Ag
               Oxidation of Cu, Reduction of Ag$^+$

○ C. Mg => Mg^{2+} + 2e$^-$
               Oxidation of Mg

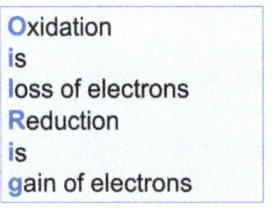

36. D
The total number of electrons shared in the bond between the **nitrogen atoms** in the azo dye molecule **below is four**.

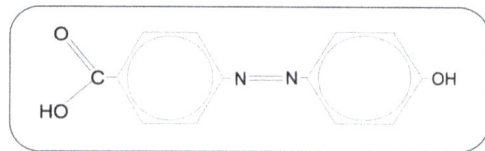

The bond between the nitrogen atoms is a *double covalent bond* which means **two electron pairs** are in the bond.

37. B
At equilibrium the concentration of **A** will be **much greater** than the concentration of **B**:

$$B \rightleftharpoons A \quad K_{eq} = [A]/[B] \quad K_{eq} = 1 \times 10^6$$

Accordingly, the **ratio** of product chemicals to reactant chemicals will be approximately **one million to one**.

38. C
As the temperature is raised the **kinetic energy** of an ideal gas molecule **increases**.

As the temperature is raised the gas molecules move faster and so have more kinetic energy.

39. B
The **Geiger counter** is used to measure radioactivity.

- A. Voltmeter is used to **measure potential difference/volts/emf**.
- C. Ammeter is used to **measure electrical current/amps**.
- D. Electron microscope is **used to observe molecular/cellular detail**.

40. C
ΔG is the **change** in **Gibbs free energy**.

G stands for Gibbs free energy.
Δ stands for *change* or *difference*.

- A. ΔS is the change in **entropy**.
- B. ΔH is the change in **enthalpy**.
- D. ΔT is the change in **temperature**.

Gibbs free energy, a measure of whether a chemical reaction will occur spontaneously, depends on entropy according to the following expression:
$$\Delta G = \Delta H + T\Delta S$$
Gibbs free energy change (ΔG) = **Enthalpy** change (ΔH) + (Absolute temperature x **Entropy** change, $T\Delta S$)

41. C
There is an **increased number of collisions between carbon and oxygen**, as there is an **increased concentration** of oxygen atoms/molecules in **pure oxygen** compared with *air which is only 21% oxygen*.

Oxygen is not more reactive at higher concentrations. Oxygen's inflammable property does not increase the rate of reaction. Oxygen does not absorb carbon dioxide.

42. A
59.5 g of potassium bromide must be added to the final 500 ml volume of solution.

To create one litre of a 1 M solution of potassium bromide, 119 g of KBr are needed.
So, for 500 ml of a 1 M solution of KBr, 119/2 = **59.5 g of potassium bromide** are needed.

43. D
Bronze is the only alloy in the list.

Bronze is an alloy (mixture) of **copper** and **tin**. Iron, copper and tin are elements.

44. D
Potassium has the biggest atomic number.

The answer options are all group IA elements - the potassium option is the lowest.

45. D
Phosphorus is not a magnetic metal.

Phosphorus is a **non-metal** and is **non-magnetic**. **Iron, cobalt and nickel** are magnetic metals.

46. C
At normal room temperature and pressure aluminium is a **solid**.

By convention, normal room temperature and pressure is **one atmosphere and 20°C**.

47. A
The reaction below is a **decomposition reaction**.
$2H_2O \Rightarrow 2H_2 + O_2$

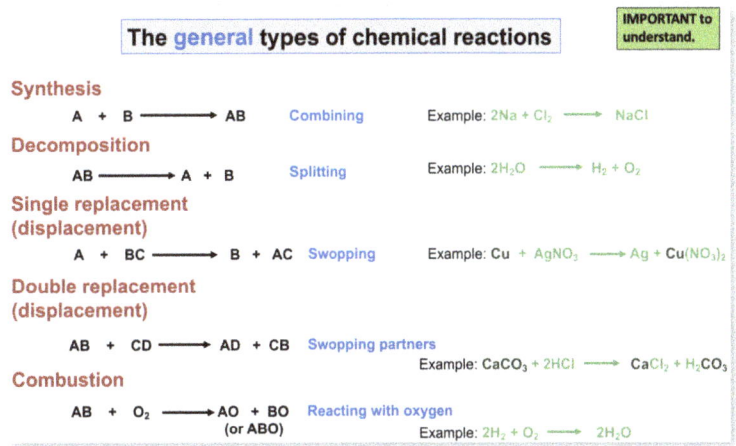

48. A
Le Chatelier's principle is used for **equilibria**.

Le Chatelier's principle states that if a stress (e.g. pressure or temperature change) is applied to an equilibrium, the equilibrium will move to try to **overcome the effect of the constraint**.

49. D
Octane is not a **carbohydrate**.

Glucose and **fructose** are carbohydrates (hexoses). **Starch** is a carbohydrate that is a polymer of the monomer *glucose*.

50. A
Fossil fuels such as coal, petroleum and natural gas all contain **hydrocarbons**.

The hydrocarbon content of these fossil fuels undergo **exothermic combustion reactions** and so **release their chemical potential energy** in a useful form.

Test Six

1. If the initial concentration of reactants for a chemical reaction is decreased, which of the following is true?

- A. The rate and final amount of product formation increases.
- B. The rate of reaction decreases.
- C. The heat of reaction decreases.
- D. The solubility of the reactants increases.

2. An *s* subshell can hold a maximum of:

- A. One electron
- B. Two electrons
- C. Three electrons
- D. Four electrons

3. In the Bohr Atom:

- A. Electrons can release light energy when they go to lower orbits.
- B. Electrons can release light energy when they go to higher orbits.
- C. Protons have a negative charge.
- D. Protons each have a mass of two atomic mass units.

4. Nickel is the element with atomic number **28**. How many neutrons and protons are contained in the nucleus of ^{59}Nickel?

- A. 31 neutrons and 27 protons
- B. 30 neutrons and 28 protons
- C. 31 neutrons and 28 protons
- D. 30 neutrons and 29 protons

5. Which of the forces between atoms is weakest?

- A. Ion-dipole.
- B. Dipole-dipole
- C. Covalent bond
- D. London dispersion

6. What type of molecule is shown below?

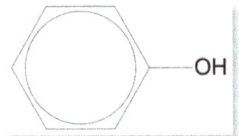

- A. A carboxylic acid
- B. An ester
- C. A phenol
- D. An ether

7. What is the molecular geometry (shape) of the carbon dioxide molecule?

- A. Trigonal
- B. Linear
- C. Circular
- D. Tetrahedral

8. Which of the following is not a solution but is a mixture?

- A. Acetic acid
- B. Water and salt
- C. Glucose and water
- D. Salt and pepper

9. How many electrons are lost or gained in this reaction: $Ca \rightarrow Ca^{2+}$?

- A. One electron is gained
- B. One electron is lost
- C. Two electrons are gained
- D. Two electrons are lost

10. Consider the following reaction. Which of the statements about this reaction is true?

$$C_5H_{12} + 8O_2 \rightarrow 5CO_2 + 6H_2O \quad \Delta H = -3000 \text{ kcal}$$

- A. This reaction is exothermic and the enthalpy is positive.
- B. This reaction is endothermic and the enthalpy is negative.
- C. This reaction is exothermic and the enthalpy is negative.
- D. This reaction is endothermic and the enthalpy is zero.

11. A solid changes state and becomes a gas. What is this process called?

- A. Sublimation
- B. Melting
- C. Evaporating
- D. Freezing

12. The copper in CuSO₄ is in which form?

- A. Cu^+
- B. Cu^{2+}
- C. Cu^{3+}
- D. Cu^{4+}

13. How much NaCl₍s₎ is needed to create 200 ml of a 3 M solution? The formula mass of NaCl₍s₎ is 58 g/mol.

- A. 34.8 g
- B. 24.8 g
- C. 14.8 g
- D. 44.8 g

14. Which of the following chemical equations is correctly balanced?

- A. $N_{2(g)} + 2H_{2(g)} \rightleftharpoons 2NH_{3(g)}$
- B. $Mg_{(s)} + 2HCl_{(aq)} \rightarrow MgCl_{2(aq)} + H_{2(g)}$
- C. $H_{2(g)} + I_{2(s)} \rightarrow HI_{(g)}$
- D. $2O_{2(g)} + CH_{4(g)} \rightarrow 2CO_{2(g)} + 2H_2O_{(l)}$

15. What are the products of the complete neutralization of nitric acid with aqueous potassium hydroxide?

- A. H₂O and HNO₃
- B. H₂O and KNO₃
- C. HNO₃ and KNO₃
- D. KCl and HNO₃

16. Which of the following is the strongest base?

- A. $NH_{3(aq)}$
- B. $Ba(OH)_{2(aq)}$
- C. $CH_3COOH_{(aq)}$
- D. $C_3H_7OH_{(aq)}$

17. What is the product X of the nuclear reaction below?

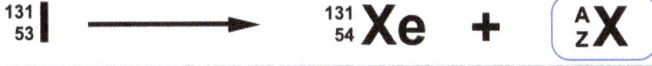

A. $^{1}_{1}H$
B. $^{131}_{54}I$
C. $^{0}_{-1}e$
D. $^{131}_{54}I$

18. $CaO_{(s)} + CO_{2(g)} \rightleftharpoons CaCO_{3(s)}$

Consider the chemical equilibrium above. What would be the result of increasing the pressure by decreasing the volume of the reaction container?

- A. The equilibrium would move to the left.
- B. The equilibrium would move to the right.
- C. There would be no effect on the equilibrium.
- D. The calcium carbonate concentration would decrease.

19. $CH_3CH_2Br + LiOH \rightarrow CH_3CH_2OH + LiBr$
What kind of organic chemistry reaction is shown above?

- A. Substitution
- B. Elimination
- C. Addition
- D. Dehydration

20. Which of the following is a popular use of the common ion effect?

- A. Creating supersaturated solutions.
- B. Salting out of soaps (precipitation of soap during manufacture).
- C. Altering the K_{sp} of a solution.
- D. Increasing the quantity of the common ion in the Earth's crust.

21. The per cent yield of a chemical reaction is:

- A. The actual yield divided by the theoretical yield, then multiplied by 100.
- B. The theoretical yield divided by the actual yield, then multiplied by 100.
- C. Not used to measure the completeness of a reaction.
- D. All of the above.

22. Which of the following is true of a buffer solution?

- A. It resists a change in temperature when small amounts of acid or alkali are added.
- B. It composed of a strong acid and a strong base.
- C. It changes colour when small amounts of acid or alkali are added to the buffer solution.
- D. It resists a change in pH when small amounts of acid or alkali are added.

23. Which chemical below is a common functional component of rechargeable batteries?

- A. Lithium ion
- B. Silver ion
- C. Aluminium ion
- D. Gold ion

24. The radioactive half-life of Iodine-131 is 8 days. How long will it take for 2 kg of Iodine-131 to decay to 500 g of Iodine-131?

- A. 4 days
- B. 8 days
- C. 16 days
- D. 32 days

25. Fluorine has an atomic number of 9 and the neutral atom has a base electronic configuration of $1s^2 2s^2 2p^5$. Which electronic configuration represents an excited fluorine atom?

- A. $1s^2 2s^2 2p^4$
- B. $1s^2 2s^2 2p^6 3s^2$
- C. $1s^2 2s^2 2p^6$
- D. $1s^2 2s^2 2p^4 3s^1$

26. Which of the following is an amino acid?

- A. glucose
- B. glycine
- C. gallium
- D. gold

27. A student has conducted a titration experiment by adding 15 ml of an unknown concentration of $Ca(OH)_{2(aq)}$ to 30 ml of 1 M $HNO_{3(aq)}$. What is the molar concentration of $Ca(OH)_{2(aq)}$?

- A. 1 M
- B. 2 M
- C. 3 M
- D. 4 M

28. Sugar is most soluble in:

- A. Olive oil
- B. Benzene
- C. Water
- D. Wax

29. If the equilibrium constant, K_{eq}, for the reaction below is 1 x 10^{-6} then which of the statements is true?

$$B \rightleftharpoons A$$

- A. At equilibrium the concentration of B will be much greater than the concentration of A.
- B. At equilibrium the concentration of A will be much greater than the concentration of B.
- C. At equilibrium the concentration of B will be equal to the concentration of A.
- D. At equilibrium 75% of the chemical mixture will be B and 25% will be A.

30. Which of the following is the most reactive element?

- A. Krypton
- B. Radon
- C. Sodium
- D. Argon

31. An ideal gas inside a closed rigid container is at constant temperature. If the number of moles of gas inside the container is increased:

- A. The pressure increases.
- B. The pressure does not change.
- C. The volume decreases.
- D. The pressure decreases.

32. Which is the term for a change of state from a liquid to gas?

- A. Freezing
- B. Condensation
- C. Deposition
- D. Vaporization

33. Which of the following chemicals does not have a linear molecular shape (linear geometry)?

- A. PCl_3
- B. H_2
- C. $HC\equiv CH$
- D. CO_2

34. Which of the following elements is most chemically similar to calcium?

- A. Silicon
- B. Lithium
- C. Titanium
- D. Magnesium

35. An unsaturated hydrocarbon compound must have carbon to carbon:

- A. Quadruple covalent bonds
- B. Double or triple covalent bonds
- C. Single covalent bonds
- D. Ionic bonds

36. Propane contains _____ carbon atoms.

- A. 1
- B. 2
- C. 3
- D. 4

37. The anion F^- is called:

- A. Fluoride
- B. Ferric
- C. Ferrous
- D. Flerovium

38. A mole of any ideal gas occupies approximately 22.4 L at standard temperature and pressure (0 °C and 1 atm). The molar mass of fluorine gas, F_2, is 38 g/mol. What is the volume occupied by 76 g of $F_{2(g)}$ at 0 °C and 1 atm?

- A. 22.4 L
- B. 67.2 L
- C. 112 L
- D. 44.8 L

39. Methylated spirits (denatured alcohol) are used as industrial and household cleaning fluids. Methylated spirits are a mixture of methanol and ethanol. If a 500 ml bottle of methylated spirits has 5% by volume of methanol, what is the volume of ethanol in the bottle?

- A. 400 ml
- B. 425 ml
- C. 450 ml
- D. 475 ml

40. Which of the following will be most attracted to a positively charged plate?

- A. Alpha particles
- B. Electrons
- C. Hydrogen atoms

○ D. Neutrons

41. Which of the following is not an alloy?

○ A. Brass
○ B. Copper
○ C. Amalgam
○ D. Bronze

42. Which of the following processes involve a chemical reaction?

○ A. Making lemonade from lemon juice and sparkling/carbonated water.
○ B. Using petrol to power your Rolls Royce car.
○ C. Mixing acetone and water to make nail varnish remover.
○ D. Making salt water.

43. Copper is above platinum in the redox activity series for metals in water. Which of the reactions below is most likely to occur?

○ A. Pt + CuSO₄ => PtSO₄ + Cu
○ B. Cu + PtSO₄ => CuSO₄ + Pt
○ C. CuCl₂ + Pt => Cu + PtCl₂
○ D. Pt + Cu(NO₃)₂ => Pt(NO₃)₂ + Cu

44.

$$N_2 + 3H_2 \underset{\text{Endothermic}}{\overset{\text{Exothermic}}{\rightleftharpoons}} 2NH_3$$

For the equilibrium above, what would happen if you increased the quantity of H_2?

○ A. The reaction equilibrium would move to the right.
○ B. The reaction equilibrium would move to the left.
○ C. The reaction equilibrium would not change.
○ D. The quantity of H_2 would decrease.

45. A **dm³** is a measure of:

○ A. Energy
○ B. Mass
○ C. Volume
○ D. Pressure

46. In which family does the element calcium belong?

- A. Transition elements
- B. Alkaline earth metals
- C. Alkali metals
- D. Inert gases

47. A car powered by petrol and containing 350 kg mass of people accelerates from 0 to 40 miles per hour. The car has:

- A. Converted chemical energy to kinetic energy.
- B. Converted electrical energy into kinetic energy.
- C. Converted chemical energy into solar power.
- D. Converted electrical energy into sound energy.

48. Which of the compounds below is a strong acid?

- A. $CH_3COOH_{(aq)}$
- B. $HCOOH_{(aq)}$
- C. $HNO_{3(aq)}$
- D. $H_2CO_{3(aq)}$

49. Calculate the mass percentage of sulphur in this compound: H_2SO_4
(Atomic masses: O = 16, S = 32, H = 1)

- A. 22%
- B. 33%
- C. 44%
- D. 55%

50. $CH_3CH=CH_2 + H_2 \rightarrow CH_3CH_2CH_3$
What kind of organic chemistry reaction is shown above?

- A. Addition
- B. Elimination
- C. Substitution
- D. Hydration

TEST SIX

ANSWER SECTION

Test Six - Answer Key									
1)	B	11)	A	21)	A	31)	A	41)	B
2)	B	12)	B	22)	D	32)	D	42)	B
3)	A	13)	A	23)	A	33)	A	43)	B
4)	C	14)	B	24)	C	34)	D	44)	A
5)	D	15)	B	25)	D	35)	B	45)	C
6)	C	16)	B	26)	B	36)	C	46)	B
7)	B	17)	C	27)	A	37)	A	47)	A
8)	D	18)	B	28)	C	38)	D	48)	C
9)	D	19)	A	29)	A	39)	D	49)	B
10)	C	20)	B	30)	C	40)	B	50)	A

1. **B**
If the concentration of reactants **decreases** in a chemical reaction, the rate of reaction **decreases**.

This is because there will be fewer reactants to collide and fewer molecules with sufficient energy to overcome the reaction activation energy barrier. Accordingly, there will also be a **decrease in the number of product molecules/chemicals** as the concentration of reactants decreases. The **heat of reaction** would only decrease if there were an enthalpy change in the reaction - but the question stem does not state this. The **solubility of reactants** is constant at a specific temperature and pressure - the solubility of reactants will not change with decreasing reactant concentrations.

2. **B**
An **s** subshell can hold a maximum of **two electrons**.

s subshell => maximum of two electrons.
p subshell => maximum of six electrons.
d subshell => maximum of ten electrons.
f subshell => maximum of fourteen electrons.

3. **A**
In the Bohr Atom model electrons can **release light** energy when they go to **lower orbits**.

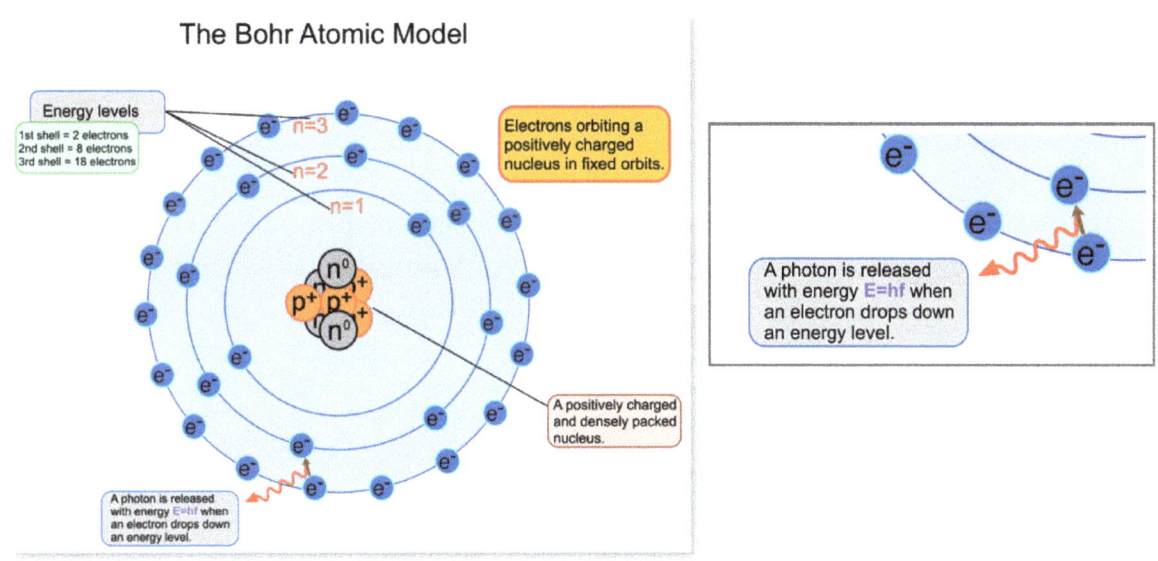

Protons have a **positive** charge. Protons each have a mass of **one atomic mass** unit.

4. **C**
31 neutrons and 28 protons are contained in the nucleus of ^{59}Nickel.

In ^{59}Nickel the **59** refers to the **mass number** (the total number of protons and neutrons in the nickel atom). The question stem also tells us that the atomic number is 28, meaning that the number of **protons** in the neutral nickel atom is **28**. So, 59 minus 28 leaves **31 neutrons** in the nickel atom.

Atomic number 27 refers to the element **cobalt** not nickel. Atomic number 29 refers to the element **copper** not nickel.

Type of bond	Bond strength
van der Waals force / London dispersion	0.1 - 4 kJ/mol
Dipole - dipole bond	5 - 20 kJ/mol
Hydrogen bond	4 - 50 kJ/mol
Ion - dipole bond	40 - 600 kJ/mol
Covalent bond	60 - 600 kJ/mol
Ionic bonds	560 - 1000 kJ/mol

5. D
The **London dispersion** force is the **weakest** interatomic force.

The London dispersion force is most significant in **nonpolar uncharged molecules**. The movement of the **electron clouds** in such a molecule can cause a **temporary dipole**. This can then cause a temporary dipole in a nearby molecule. Finally, the weak force of attraction between these **two adjacent temporary dipoles** is called the London dispersion force.

6. C
The shown molecule is **phenol** (the hydroxyl group is directly attached to the benzene ring).

The other molecular options are shown below:

7. B
The molecular geometry (shape) of the **carbon dioxide** molecule is **linear**.

This molecule is organized by its covalent bonds to keep the electronegative oxygen atoms as far apart as possible:

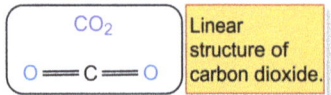

8. D
Salt and pepper together make a **mixture**.

Salt and pepper are solids and so cannot form a solution. They can only form **a mixture**.
Acetic acid is a pure *single* compound and so is **not a mixture**. If the acetic acid were in water then it would be **a solution** of acetic acid in water. Water and salt together will form a solution. Glucose and water together also form a solution.

9. D
Two electrons are lost from the calcium atom during this reaction: $Ca \rightarrow Ca^{2+}$.

$Ca \rightarrow Ca^{2+} + 2e^-$

The calcium atom is *oxidized* as part of this redox reaction.

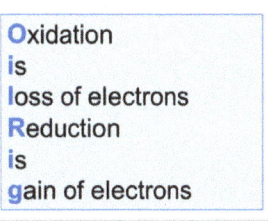

Oxidation
is
loss of electrons
Reduction
is
gain of electrons

10. C
This reaction is **exothermic** and the **enthalpy is negative**:
$C_5H_{12} + 8O_2 \rightarrow 5CO_2 + 6H_2O \quad \Delta H = -3000\ kcal$

This is because exothermic reactions have negative enthalpy, by definition.

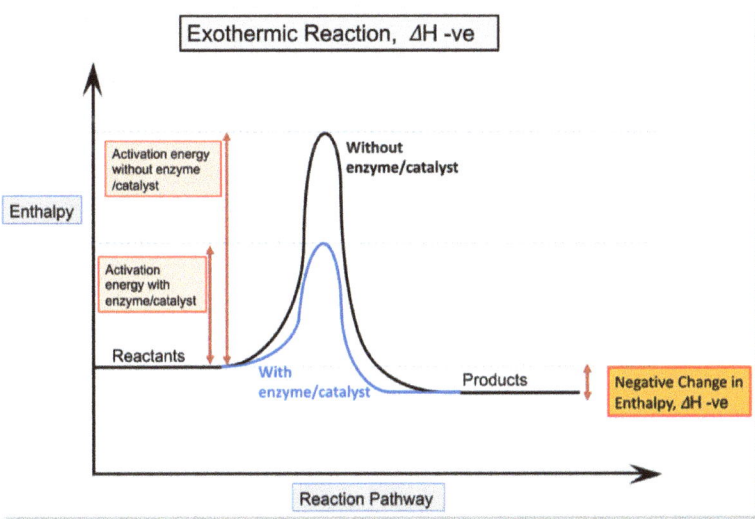

11. A
A solid changes state and becomes a gas. This is **sublimation**:

Phase Change	Example	Terminology (Name)
solid to liquid	Ice to water.	Melting
liquid to gas	Water to steam (water vapour).	Evaporation / Vaporization
solid to gas	1) Iodine solid to iodine vapour. 2) Dry ice (solid CO_2) to carbon dioxide gas.	Sublimation
gas to liquid	Condensation that occurs to cause rain.	Condensation
liquid to solid	Freezing of water to form ice on a cold day.	Freezing
gas to solid	Water vapour forming frost on a window.	Deposition

12. B
The **copper** in $CuSO_4$ is in the form of Cu^{2+}.

Because SO_4^{2-} has **two negative charges** and the whole chemical, $CuSO_4$, is neutrally charged then the **copper ion** must have **two positive charges** to balance and match the charge on the sulphate ion. The **+2 valency** is the commonest valency of the copper cation.

13. A
34.8 g of $NaCl_{(s)}$ is needed to create 200 ml of a 3 M solution.

The **formula mass** of $NaCl_{(s)}$ is **58 g/mol**.
3 moles of $NaCl_{(s)}$ => 3 x 58 g = 174 g
3 M $NaCl_{(s)}$ solution in 1 litre of fluid => 174 g in 1 litre
3 M $NaCl_{(s)}$ solution in 200 ml of fluid => 174/5 = **34.8 g**

14. B
This chemical equation is correctly **balanced**: $Mg_{(s)} + 2HCl_{(aq)} \rightarrow MgCl_{2(aq)} + H_{2(g)}$

Left side of the chemical equation: **Mg**   Right side of the chemical equation: **Mg**
                                     2H   **2H**
                                     2Cl   **2Cl**

The number of atoms of each type is the same on both sides of the chemical equation *so the chemical reaction is balanced*.

The chemical equations below are now correctly balanced:

○ A. $N_{2(g)} + 3H_{2(g)} \rightleftharpoons 2NH_{3(g)}$

○ C. $H_{2(g)} + I_{2(s)} \rightarrow 2HI_{(g)}$

○ D. $2O_{2(g)} + CH_{4(g)} \rightarrow CO_{2(g)} + 2H_2O_{(l)}$

15. B
The products of the complete neutralization of nitric acid with aqueous potassium hydroxide are H_2O and KNO_3:

$HNO_3 + KOH \rightarrow KNO_3 + H_2O$ (Acid + Base → Salt and Water)

This is a **double replacement/displacement** reaction.

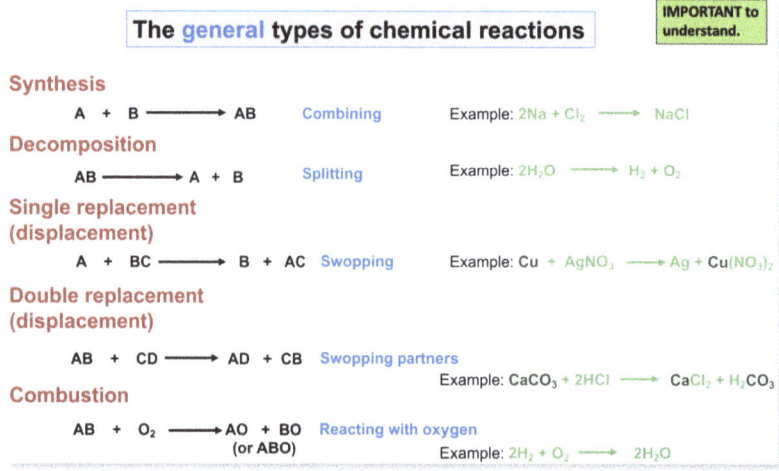

16. B
Ba(OH)$_{2(aq)}$ is the **strongest base** amongst the answer options.

When each of the compounds is mixed with water, barium hydroxide produces the most **hydroxide ions**:

$Ba(OH)_2 + H_2O \rightarrow Ba^{2+} + 2OH^-$

$NH_3 + H_2O \rightleftharpoons NH_4^+ + OH^-$

$CH_3COOH + H_2O \rightleftharpoons CH_3COO^- + H_3O^+$

$C_3H_7OH + H_2O \rightleftharpoons C_3H_7O^- + H_3O^+$

The **barium hydroxide reaction** moves to **near completion** in water and so most of the barium hydroxide takes the form of **barium ions** and **hydroxide ions** (the reaction is far to the right of the chemical equation above). In contrast, the other three reactions are either equilibria or are far to the left as written.

17. C
X is an **electron**:

$^{131}_{53}I \longrightarrow \, ^{131}_{54}Xe + \, ^{0}_{-1}e$

The particle **X** can be deduced by subtracting 131 from 131 to make **zero**.
And then by subtracting 54 from 53 to make **-1**.
The result is a negatively **charged particle with essentially no mass**, this is the **electron**.

18. B
The equilibrium would move to the **right**:
$CaO_{(s)} + CO_{2(g)} \rightleftharpoons CaCO_{3(s)}$

This answer can be reached by following Le Chatelier's principle. The equilibrium must move to remove the effect of the increased pressure:

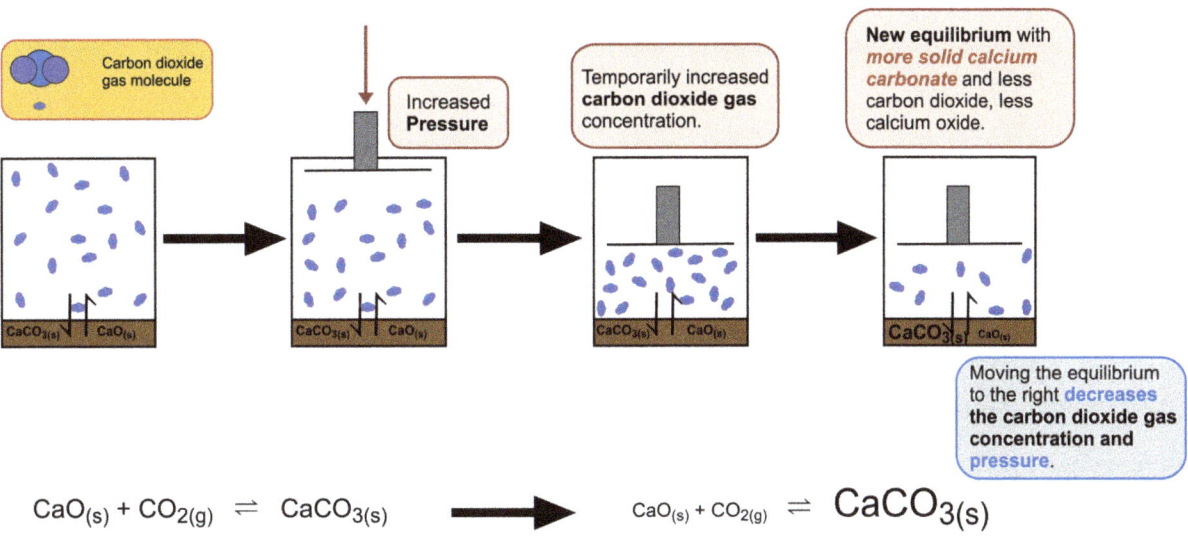

$CaO_{(s)} + CO_{2(g)} \rightleftharpoons CaCO_{3(s)} \longrightarrow CaO_{(s)} + CO_{2(g)} \rightleftharpoons CaCO_{3(s)}$

Increasing pressure shifts the equilibrium to the right to decrease the carbon dioxide gas pressure (Le Chatelier's Principle).

19. A
The organic chemistry reaction shown below is a **substitution** reaction.
$CH_3CH_2\mathbf{Br} + LiOH \rightarrow CH_3CH_2\mathbf{OH} + LiBr$

The **bromine** atom in the ethyl bromide is swopped or *substituted* for the **hydroxyl (OH)** group during this reaction.

20. B
Salting out of soaps (precipitation of soap during manufacture) is a popular use of the *common ion effect*.

Consider the equilibrium:
1) $RCOO^-Na^+_{(s)} \rightleftharpoons RCOO^-_{(aq)} + Na^+_{(aq)}$ $RCOO^-Na^+$ is the general formula for **soap**.

If NaCl is added to this aqueous reaction mixture, the NaCl will dissociate to become ions:
2) $NaCl_{(s)} \rightarrow Na^+_{(aq)} + Cl^-_{(aq)}$

Notice that the sodium **ion is common** to both reaction (1) and reaction (2). The added sodium ions from reaction (2) affect the equilibrium in (1) and push this reaction to the left:

$\mathbf{RCOO^-Na^+_{(s)}} \rightleftharpoons RCOO^-_{(aq)} + Na^+_{(aq)}$
⟵

> The added sodium ions cause precipitation of RCOONa by moving the equilibrium to the left.

Because the sodium ions cause the **precipitation of RCOONa**, this process can be used to **precipitate soap** out of solution as part of the chemical synthesis of soap.

So, the *common ion effect* is an application of Le Chatelier's principle.

21. A
The **per cent yield** is the *actual yield divided by the theoretical yield*, then multiplied by 100.

For example:

Glucose + Oxygen → Carbon dioxide + Water
$C_6H_{12}O_6 + 6O_2 \rightarrow 6CO_2 + 6H_2O$
   1   6   6   6

So, **one mole** of glucose should produce **six moles** of carbon dioxide or water, for a 100% yield. If in reality, **only five moles of carbon dioxide** were produced from one mole of glucose then the yield for this reaction would be:

% Yield = (5/6) x 100 = 83%

22. D
A **buffer solution** resists a change in pH when **small amounts of acid or alkali** are added.

Buffer solutions are equilibria involving weak acids in water (an acidic buffer) or equilibria of weak bases in water (alkaline buffer). If a small amount of acid is added to an acidic buffer then the pH only decreases slightly because most of the hydrogen ions are absorbed and removed from solution. For example:
$CH_3COOH_{(l)} \rightleftharpoons CH_3COO^-_{(aq)} + H^+_{(aq)}$

If more hydrogen ions are added to the above equilibrium they will bind to the ethanoate to form ethanoic acid molecules and mostly remain as ethanoic acid in this equilibrium. Similar reasoning applies to the addition of hydroxyl ions. There are analogous explanations for adding an acid or a base to an alkaline buffer. **Buffers are not designed to resist temperature changes nor are all buffers designed to change colour**.

23. **A**
Lithium ions are important in the function of rechargeable batteries.

This is because lithium ions are *an efficient electrolyte* that move between the anode and cathode of the rechargeable battery.

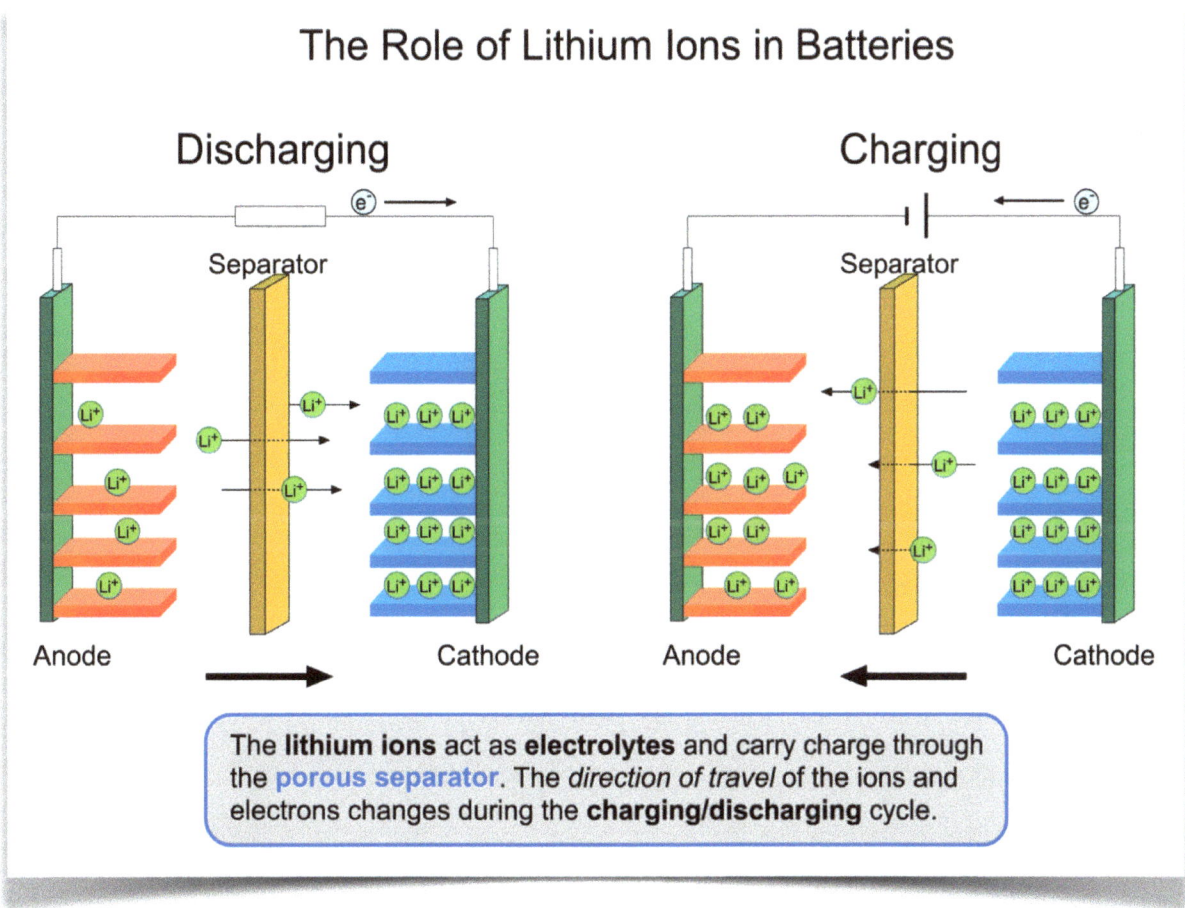

24. **C**
It will take **16 days** for 2 kg of Iodine-131 to decay to 500 g of Iodine-131.

The definition of half-life is the time taken for half the number of radioactive nuclides originally present to disintegrate. So, after eight days the quantity of Iodine-131 atoms will drop from 2 kg/2000 grams to 1 kg/1000 grams. After a further eight days the quantity of Iodine-131 atoms will drop from 1 kg/1000 grams to 0.5 kg/500 grams.

Radioactive decay can also be calculated using the expression below:
$$N = N_0 e^{-\lambda t}$$

N_o is the initial quantity of radioactive nuclides, N is the final quantity of radioactive nuclides, λ is the decay constant, t is elapsed time (time allowed for decay) and e is the Euler constant 2.71828.

25. D
The **electronic configuration** $1s^2 2s^2 2p^4 3s^1$ represents an excited fluorine atom.
Because fluorine has an atomic number of nine the neutral atom must have nine electrons, but an excited fluorine atom does not have all the electrons in the base state. In an excited atom at least one electron must be elevated to a higher energy subshell.

- ○ A. $1s^2 2s^2 2p^4$ => atomic number 8 for **carbon**.
- ○ B. $1s^2 2s^2 2p^6 3s^2$ => atomic number 12 for **magnesium**.
- ○ C. $1s^2 2s^2 2p^6$ => atomic number 10 for **neon**.
- ○ D. $1s^2 2s^2 2p^4 3s^1$ => **atomic number 9 with an electron excited to the *s* subshell.**

26. B
Glycine is an amino acid.

An **amino acid** is the **monomer** (single building block) of a protein or a polypeptide. As the name suggests the amino acid has at least one **amine functional group** and one **carboxylic acid** functional group:

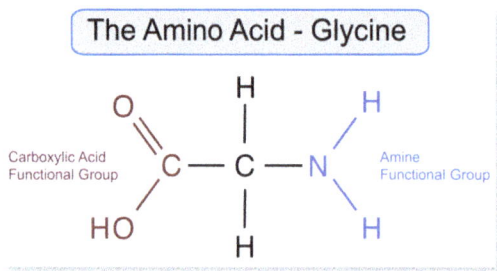

Glucose is a monomer of a polysaccharide. **Gold** and **gallium** are elements not compounds.

27. A
The molar concentration of $Ca(OH)_{2(aq)}$ is **1 M**.

$$Ca(OH)_{2(aq)} + 2HNO_{3(aq)} => Ca(NO_3)_{2(aq)} + 2H_2O_{(l)}$$
$$\;\;\;\;\;\;1 \;\;\;\;\;\;\;\;\;\;\;\;\;\; 2 \;\;\;\;\;\;\;\;\;\;\;\;\;\;\;\;\;\;\; 1 \;\;\;\;\;\;\;\;\;\;\;\;\; 2 \;\;\;\; (Stoichiometry)$$

So, for this complete titration reaction **15 ml** of **1 molar calcium hydroxide** are required to neutralize **30 ml** of **1 molar nitric acid**, in order to balance this reaction. In this way there will be twice as much nitric acid present as calcium hydroxide, in agreement with the stoichiometry of the reaction.

28. C
Sugar is most soluble in **water**.

In chemistry the simplest rule regarding solubility is that "*like dissolves like.*" Sugar is a **polar** molecule (**fructose**) and **water** is a **polar** solvent (H_2O) and so they tend to mix and dissolve well. In fact, sugar can even *hydrogen bond* with the water. In contrast olive oil, wax and benzene are relatively nonpolar solvents and so do not dissolve sugar well.

29. A

At equilibrium the concentration of **B** will be **much greater** than the concentration of **A**:

$$B \rightleftharpoons A \qquad K_{eq} = [A]/[B] \qquad K_{eq} = 1 \times 10^{-6}$$

The **ratio** of reactant chemicals to product chemicals will be approximately **one million to one**.
The value of the **equilibrium constant is so small** that the equilibrium has shifted far to the left of the reaction above and so nearly all the chemicals present will be reactants.

30. C

Sodium is the most reactive element.

Radon, krypton and argon are inert, unreactive noble gases. In contrast, sodium is a very reactive group IA metal that donates one outer subshell electron during its reactions.

Atomic number, Z	Element	Number of electrons/shell	Comment
18	Argon	2, 8, 8	Complete and stable outer subshell.
36	Krypton	2, 8, 18, 8	Complete and stable outer subshell.
86	Radon	2, 8, 18, 32, 18, 8	Complete and stable outer subshell.
11	Sodium	2, 8, 1	Incomplete outer subshell that stabilizes by electron donation.

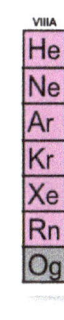

31. A

The **pressure** inside the container **increases**.

An ideal gas will obey the **ideal gas equation**:

$$PV = nRT$$

P = pressure of the gas
V = volume of the gas
n = number of moles of the gas
R = universal/ideal gas constant
T = temperature of the gas (in Kelvin)

As the rigid container has a constant volume and the temperature is constant any increase in the number of moles of gas (**n**) will increase the pressure (**P**). In this scenario the ***pressure is directly proportional to the number of moles of gas***.

32. D

The term for a change of state from a liquid to gas is **vaporization**:

Phase Change	Example	Terminology (Name)
solid to liquid	Ice to water.	Melting
liquid to gas	Water to steam (water vapour).	Evaporation / Vaporization
solid to gas	1) Iodine solid to iodine vapour. 2) Dry ice (solid CO_2) to carbon dioxide gas.	Sublimation
gas to liquid	Condensation that occurs to cause rain.	Condensation
liquid to solid	Freezing of water to form ice on a cold day.	Freezing
gas to solid	Water vapour forming frost on a window.	Deposition

33. A
PCl₃, phosphorus trichloride, does **not have a linear molecular shape**:

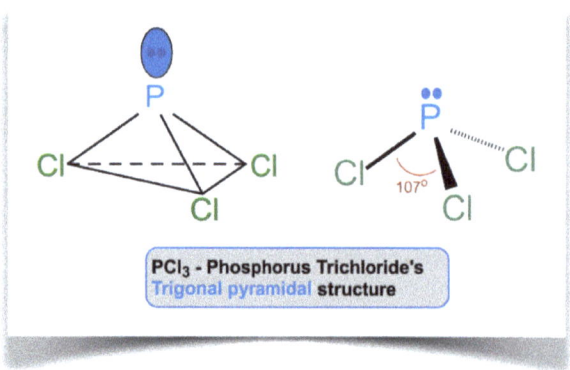

Ethyne (HC≡CH), hydrogen (H_2) and carbon dioxide (CO_2) molecules have linear molecular shapes.

34. D
Magnesium is most chemically similar to **calcium**.

Elements in the same group of the periodic table have similar chemical properties. Both calcium and magnesium are group IIA (alkaline earth metals).

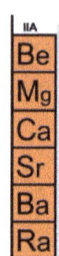

35. B
An **unsaturated hydrocarbon** compound contains **carbon to carbon double or triple bonds**.

A *saturated* hydrocarbon compound contains single bonds between carbon atoms. An unsaturated hydrocarbon is the opposite of this and so contains carbon atom to carbon atom double or triple bonds.

36. C
Propane contains **three carbon** atoms.

This is the beginning of the **alkane homologous series**:

Name of straight chain alkane		Number of carbon atoms
Methane	CH_4	One
Ethane	C_2H_6	Two
Propane	C_3H_8	Three
Butane	C_4H_{10}	Four
Pentane	C_5H_{12}	Five
Hexane	C_6H_{14}	Six
Heptane	C_7H_{16}	Seven
Octane	C_8H_{18}	Eight
Nonane	C_9H_{20}	Nine
Decane	$C_{10}H_{22}$	Ten

37. A
The F^- anion is called **fluoride**.

○ B. Ferric => Fe^{3+}
○ C. Ferrous => Fe^{2+}
○ D. Flerovium => Fl

38. D
The volume occupied by 76 g of $F_{2(g)}$ at 0 °C and 1 atm is **44.8 L**.

As a mole of any ideal gas occupies approximately 22.4 L at standard temperature and pressure (0 °C and 1 atm), then 2 moles (76 g/38 g) must have a volume of **2 x 22.4 = 44.8 L**.
This and similar questions assume that fluorine is an ideal gas.

39. D
The **volume** of ethanol in the bottle is **475 ml**.

The methylated spirits are a mixture of methanol and ethanol only. If **5% by volume** is methanol then the ethanol percentage by volume must be **95%**.
To calculate the *volume* of ethanol:
95% x 500 ml => **475 ml**

40. B
Electrons will be most attracted to a **positively charged plate**.

Because electrons are **negatively charged** they will be most attracted to the **positive charge**.
In contrast, neutrons and hydrogen atoms are neutral in charge. Alpha particles are positively charged and will be repelled from a positively charged plate.

41. B
Copper is an element **not an alloy**.

An alloy is a **mixture of metals** - it is a physical mixture.

Examples of alloys include:

Brass = copper and zinc.
Bronze = copper and tin.
Amalgam = mercury and another metal.

42. B
Using petrol to power your car involves **a chemical reaction**.

The petrol in a car undergoes *exothermic* **combustion** to power the **combustion engine**. This is an oxidation chemical reaction. The other options are **physical mixtures** not chemical reactions.

43. B
$Cu + PtSO_4 => CuSO_4 + Pt$ is the most likely reaction to occur.

As copper is higher up than platinum in the **redox activity series** in aqueous solution, copper will be oxidized and platinum ions will be reduced. Only reaction **(B)** describes oxidized copper and reduced platinum ions.

The Redox Activity Series		
$Li_{(s)} \Rightarrow Li^+_{(aq)} + e^-$	Oxidation reaction	*Increasing ease of oxidation* ↑
$K_{(s)} \Rightarrow K^+_{(aq)} + e^-$	Oxidation reaction	
$Ba_{(s)} \Rightarrow Ba^{2+}_{(aq)} + 2e^-$	Oxidation reaction	
$Ca_{(s)} \Rightarrow Ca^{2+}_{(aq)} + 2e^-$	Oxidation reaction	
$Mg_{(s)} \Rightarrow Mg^{2+}_{(aq)} + 2e^-$	Oxidation reaction	
$Zn_{(s)} \Rightarrow Zn^{2+}_{(aq)} + 2e^-$	Oxidation reaction	
$Fe_{(s)} \Rightarrow Fe^{2+}_{(aq)} + 2e^-$	Oxidation reaction	
$Cu_{(s)} \Rightarrow Cu^{2+}_{(aq)} + 2e^-$	Oxidation reaction	
$Ag_{(s)} \Rightarrow Ag^{2+}_{(aq)} + 2e^-$	Oxidation reaction	
$Pt_{(s)} \Rightarrow Pt^{2+}_{(aq)} + 2e^-$		

44. A
The **reaction equilibrium** would move to the **right**.

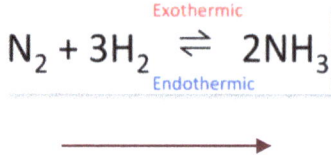

According to Le Chatelier's principle, the equilibrium will move to remove the additional hydrogen. So, more nitrogen will combine with the hydrogen to make more ammonia.

45. C
dm³ is a measure of **volume**.

The notation **dm³** means *decimetre cubed* or *cubic decimetre*. Like **cc** (**centimetre cubed**) this is a measure of volume.

46. B
Calcium is an **alkaline earth metal**.

47. A
The car has converted **chemical energy** into **kinetic energy**.

The **chemical energy** stored in petroleum is released during combustion to power the car engine and cause movement. Movement is **kinetic energy**. There is no conversion to **solar power**. There is no original **electrical energy** (the energy is originally in the form of *chemical* potential energy).

48. C
The strongest acid is **nitric acid, $HNO_{3(aq)}$**.

A strong acid is one that shows near complete dissociation into hydrogen/hydronium ions and a conjugate base. Only nitric acid does this. The other acids do not completely dissociate but instead form equilibria:

$CH_3COOH_{(aq)} \rightleftharpoons CH_3COO^-_{(aq)} + H^+_{(aq)}$ $K_a = 1.76 \times 10^{-5}$

$HCOOH_{(aq)} \rightleftharpoons HCOO^-_{(aq)} + H^+_{(aq)}$ $K_a = 1.8 \times 10^{-4}$

$H_2CO_{3(aq)} \rightleftharpoons HCO_3^-_{(aq)} + H^+_{(aq)}$ $K_a = 4.3 \times 10^{-7}$

$HNO_{3(aq)} \rightarrow NO_3^-_{(aq)} + H^+_{(aq)}$ $K_a = 2.3 \times 10^{1}$

Accordingly, the **dissociation constant, K_a,** of nitric acid is **much greater** than the dissociation constant of the other **weak acids**.

49. B
The mass percentage of **sulphur** in H_2SO_4 is **33%**.

It can be calculated:

(Atomic masses: H = 1, S = 32, O = 16)
Atomic mass of sulphur is **32**.
Formula mass/Molar mass of H_2SO_4 is 2 + 32 + (16 × 4) = **98**
Mass percentage of sulphur = 32/98 = **33%**

50. A
The reaction is an **addition** reaction:
$CH_3CH=CH_2 + H_2 \rightarrow CH_3CH_2CH_3$

Addition reactions add atoms across double or single bonds to make them less unsaturated.
Elimination reactions are the opposite of addition reactions and so create double or triple bonds.

www.ingramcontent.com/pod-product-compliance
Lightning Source LLC
Chambersburg PA
CBHW061140230426
43663CB00027B/2988